'Brewster and Morgan dare to enter this powerful conversation in exploring the assumptions and challenges about race. Dialoguing from within their own cultural, social-political context exploring European and African diaspora histories as Jungian analysts, they consider the intergenerational context and its relevance for us today. In this important text they create a rich psychological space in which to meet, reflect and share experiences finding a soulful meeting place. This important discussion invites us to re-think and critically interrogate our shared histories, collective memories, psychic disenfranchisement, through radical honesty and to encounter each other through opening dialogue.'

Anthea Benjamin, *Psychotherapist, Supervisor and Group Analyst UKCP & BACP registered*

'This is a brilliant and creative piece of work that examines raciality from an Africanist and White perspective. It is also an act of empowerment and response to Jung excising the black experience. A self-identified Africanist, Fanny Brewster, PhD centers Africanist traditions and the healing arts in the treatment room. She takes us on a journey of mapping out her ancestral origins with imaginings of her ancestor standing on a pier. Her poem to her ancestor took my breath away. We are reminded that we are not outside of history as we live these horrors today. This is a valuable model of how to weave cultural Africanist traditions, spirituality and history in an analytic psychological treatment.'

Rossanna Echegoyén, *LCSW, Founder and Co-Chair of the Committee for Race and Ethnicity at the Manhattan Institute for Psychoanalysis*

'*Racial Legacies* is the poetic and scholarly outcome of a deep, courageous, transatlantic engagement with racial complex by Fanny Brewster and Helen Morgan. This is an essential book for 21st century Jungians, with two distinct voices to guide engagement with systems of racism and white privilege and their implications for the theory and practice of Analytical Psychology.'

Jane Johnson, *Senior member British Psychotherapy Foundation and British Jungian Analytic Association*

'In this unique work, Brewster and Morgan collaborate to intertwine their voices and stories – reaching across the Atlantic bringing the different UK and US cultures into the mix – in the service of exploring our relationships to race. Brewster and Morgan take the field to the cutting edge of where and how analysts need to be addressing race head on in the era following the murder of George Floyd. Their dialogue models respectful interaction while confronting history, theory and politics head on. They rightly alert us: "In our contemporary practice of psychology we must be aware of the racialized foundations of Modern Psychology." Brewster alerts us: "The voice of members of the African Diaspora when expressed says that the whiteness of psychoanalysis does not see them, cannot see them and include their cultural identity of blackness." If Jungian analysis is to dig itself out of its at times racist silo, it needs to pay attention to this book. The authors challenge us to have "sufficient confidence in the robustness of the core principles of psychoanalytic and Jungian analytic theory to trust that they can withstand some rattling." The book ends by turning back on itself to provide a meta view of the writing and process of managing the intrinsic challenges of co-writing from both a black and a white perspective which is profoundly honest, transparent and moving. A model for us all.'

Ruth Williams, *Jungian Training and Supervising Analyst (AJA).*
Author of Jung: The Basics *(Routledge 2019)*

'Jungian Analysts Fanny Brewster, an African American Black and Helen Morgan, a Caucasian from England joined in a courageous endeavor to explore the complexities of racism, politics, culture and psychology. Through their trust, mistrust, struggles and openness they display a willingness and vulnerability to hold different perspectives while continuing to talk. This book is a recommended read for those who are interested in understanding how to hold different perspectives while engaging in heartfelt conversations around difficult subject matter. The authors open conversations provide a psychological model that can improve racial relationships and help create a future just society.'

Jane Selinske, *Ed.D., LCSW, NCPsyA, President*
C. G. Jung Foundation for Analytic Psychology, NY

'I find myself between loud applause and profound sadness and tears as I finish reading *Racial Legacies: Jung, Politics and Culture*. I am in tears of white guilt, of compassion for the years and years of personal and political struggle on the part of black people. Fanny Brewster and Helen Morgan clarify a picture of how hard it is to address systemic racism without an empathic understanding of the centuries of greed, torture, white power and unconsciousness suffered by Africanist people, particularly in the south of the United States. In her book, *Caste*, Isabel Wilkerson talks of class consciousness as "the worn grooves of comforting routines and unthinking expectations, patterns of a social order that have been in place for so long that (they) look like the natural order of things." It is this cruel complacency that Jungian psychology has the potential to expose by helping to make clear the power of unconscious archetypes, such as equating whiteness with goodness and righteousness, blackness with evil and badness. How long must we wait?'

Elizabeth Stevenson, *M.Div. Jungian Psychoanalyst*

'Every few years, a book comes along that revitalizes, restores, renews our faith in womankind, taking us by the hand, leading us into the dream world of our collective past from which we emerge more wholly ourselves – which is, *Racial Legacies: Jung, Politics and Culture*. Generous, precise and unsentimental, Fanny Brewster and Helen Morgan offer a brilliant collaboration that achieves this and more. Brewster and Morgan have created a deeply personal and moving book, perfectly suited for the times we are living, the authors compare their own ethnic backgrounds with others to create a "sharing space" of enlightenment ... A thought-provoking must read book.'

Dianne Travis-Teague, *Director, Alumni Relations, Pacifica Graduate Institute*

'What a wonderful idea to bring disparate voices together to explore how each approaches the history and experience of cultural differences within the field of psychoanalysis. *Racial Legacies: Jung, Politics and Culture* by Fanny Brewster and Helen Morgan provides a thoughtful, fresh discussion of the presence of *the Other* both within and outside of the consulting room. Recounting their individual experiences of their own races in childhood, Brewster and Morgan go on to examine and compare their first notable encounters with *others* from different ethnic and cultural backgrounds and share their "wonderment and concern" for race in analytic relationships.'

Beth Boardman, *RN, MA, PhD, Lecturer, Mythologist, Author, Chair, PGIAA Advisory Board*

Racial Legacies

This essential new book presents a discussion of racial relations, Jungian psychology and politics as a dialogue between two Jungian analysts of different nationalities and ethnicities, providing insight into a previously unexplored area of Jungian psychology.

Racial Legacies explores themes and historical events from the perspective of each author, and through the lens of psychology, politics and race, in the hopes of creating meaningful racial relationships. The historical ways the past has affected the authors' ancestors and their own lives today is explored in detail through essays and dialogue, demonstrating that past racial legacies continue to bind on both conscious and unconscious levels.

This book distinguishes itself from other texts as the first of its kind to present a racial dialogue in the context of Jungian psychology. It will be of great value to psychoanalysts, psychotherapists and students of Depth and Analytical Psychology.

Fanny Brewster, Ph.D., M.F.A., is a Jungian analyst and Professor of Depth Psychology at Pacifica Graduate Institute, USA.

Helen Morgan is a Fellow of the British Psychotherapy Foundation and is a training analyst and supervisor for the Jungian Analytic Association within the BPF.

Routledge Focus on Jung, Politics and Culture

The *Jung, Politics and Culture* series showcases the 'political turn' in Jungian and Post-Jungian psychology. Established and emerging authors offer unique perspectives and new insights as they explore the connections between Jungian psychology and key topics – including national and international politics, gender, race and human rights.

For a full list of titles in this series, please visit www.routledge.com/Focus-on-Jung-Politics-and-Culture/book-series/FJPC

Titles in the series:

Torture Survivors in Analytic Therapy: Jung, Politics and Culture
Monica Luci

Racial Legacies: Jung, Politics and Culture
Fanny Brewster and Helen Morgan

From Vision to Folly in the American Soul: Jung, Politics and Culture
Thomas Singer

Vision, Reality and Complex: Jung, Politics and Culture
Thomas Singer

Anti-Semitism and Analytical Psychology: Jung, Politics and Culture
Daniel Burston

Racial Legacies
Jung, Politics and Culture

Fanny Brewster and Helen Morgan

LONDON AND NEW YORK

First published 2022
by Routledge
4 Park Square, Milton Park, Abingdon, Oxon OX14 4RN

and by Routledge
605 Third Avenue, New York, NY 10158

Routledge is an imprint of the Taylor & Francis Group, an informa business

© 2022 Fanny Brewster and Helen Morgan

The right of Fanny Brewster and Helen Morgan to be identified as authors of this work has been asserted in accordance with sections 77 and 78 of the Copyright, Designs and Patents Act 1988.

All rights reserved. No part of this book may be reprinted or reproduced or utilised in any form or by any electronic, mechanical, or other means, now known or hereafter invented, including photocopying and recording, or in any information storage or retrieval system, without permission in writing from the publishers.

Trademark notice: Product or corporate names may be trademarks or registered trademarks, and are used only for identification and explanation without intent to infringe.

British Library Cataloguing-in-Publication Data
A catalogue record for this book is available from the British Library

Library of Congress Cataloging-in-Publication Data
Names: Brewster, Fanny, author. | Morgan, Helen (Psychoanalyst), author.
Title: Racial legacies: Jung, politics and culture /
Fanny Brewster and Helen Morgan.
Description: Abingdon, Oxon; New York, NY: Routledge, 2022. |
Series: Focus on Jung, politics and culture |
Includes bibliographical references and index. |
Identifiers: LCCN 2021047564 | ISBN 9780367458409 (hardback) |
ISBN 9781032221496 (paperback) | ISBN 9781003025689 (ebook)
Subjects: LCSH: Race relations–Psychological aspects. | Jungian psychology.
Classification: LCC HT1523 .B74 2022 |
DDC 305.8001/9–dc23/eng/20211119
LC record available at https://lccn.loc.gov/2021047564

ISBN: 978-0-367-45840-9 (hbk)
ISBN: 978-1-032-22149-6 (pbk)
ISBN: 978-1-003-02568-9 (ebk)

DOI: 10.4324/9781003025689

Typeset in Times New Roman
by Newgen Publishing UK

Dedicated to the Ancestors who gave us life

Contents

Acknowledgments   xii

Introduction   1

1   Before the African Holocaust   15

2   Imagining Our Ancestors   33

3   The Racial Complex   50

4   The Creation of the *Other*: Modern Psychology and Its Influences   64

5   Color Matters   81

6   The Politics of Race   97

7   Concluding Thoughts   111

References   125
Index   129

Acknowledgments

I wish to thank individuals and groups from various parts of my life for their support in the writing of this book. First among individuals is Andrew Samuels who has been a valued and visionary mentor. His deep faith in this writing project has brought it to fruition.

I appreciate the conversations, group processes and warm welcome that I received at C.G. Jung Institutes of Boston, San Francisco, Denver. I thank each of these institutes for contributing to my better understanding of the material in the book and how to develop ideas that added to the integrity of the written work. We supported one another during a year of pandemic. I remember their kindness and care during this time.

Editorial leadership for this writing project has been provided by both Susannah Frearson and Alexis O'Brien. I appreciate their understanding of me as a writer and as well as their ability to provide an ongoing, nurturing space in which to create this book with Helen Morgan.

Fanny Brewster

In addition to those listed above, I would like to thank those with whom I have had significant conversations on the subject of race and racism over the years. While not always easy, they have been critical in helping to shape my thinking around this difficult but important matter. I thank them for their understanding and generosity.

Helen Morgan

Introduction

Part One Fanny Brewster

Racial Legacies: Jung, Politics and Culture shares authorship between Fanny Brewster and Helen Morgan as Jungian analysts, each living respectively within the cultural and political frames of American and British societies. This co-authorship allows both of us to peer intently, and at times with anxiety and caution, into the white and black world of ethnicity of the professional "Other." As I had learned while presenting in the London conference, where my co-author resides and where I first met her, this is rarely done—psychoanalysts of different ethnicities coming together, for professional discussions, social gathering or the sharing of ideas that affect their clinical work through conferences.

I have decided to join with Helen in creating this book of narrative dialogue because I think that there is so much that remains to be said regarding racial relations, racism and politics. The language of clinical, Analytical Psychology and broadly the field of psychology continues to oftentimes support a foundational history that is harmful to those of Africanist ancestry. This of course ripples out to all members of our cultural and global collectives. I write this book in the hope that it can be part of the necessary movement toward deepening consciousness—as a positive rewriting of psychological concepts, theories and philosophy as regards Africanist people. There are many narratives *about* black people. As a woman of African ancestry—a psychoanalyst, who sees the discrepancy within the field of Analytical Psychology, as well as racial discrepancy in the white and black lives of our collective, I choose to add my voice toward constructive change.

Helen and I have come together as writers from different ethnic backgrounds. I am of Africanist ancestry. I was born and lived my childhood years in a small coastal town in South Carolina, which had been a port for the arrival of slaves and the shipping of rice for centuries.

DOI: 10.4324/9781003025689-1

Introduction

My ancestors more than likely arrived in Charleston harbor on a slave ship from Cameroon, Congo, Mali or Nigeria. These are the countries that very recently indicate my ancestral DNA origination.

My "family" name Wragg, belonged to a British line of South Carolina Low Country rice plantation owners. Some of my ancestors are buried in the black cemetery section of the white family slave owner plantation in Charleston. The first *barony* of Wragg land was purchased by Samuel Wragg, a British citizen, in 1717. His son William Wragg later moved to Georgetown where my father's grandparents were born into slavery on the Wedgefield Plantation. The Wragg family held their Charleston, South Carolina, estate plantation and plantations in Georgetown for 150 years. Historical records show that by 1790 the barony had 200 slaves.

At Fort Sumter in Charleston in April 1861, the sound of cannon fire shot in defense of the Confederacy signaled the beginning of the end of 300 years of slavery. The Civil War and its near destruction of Charleston saw the end of the Wragg estate, as it had been preserved for all the years of plantation slavery. My parents, their parents, my great-grandparents and all the family before survived, lived and died in the reality and historical shadow of Southern plantation slavery in the Low Country between Charleston and Georgetown, South Carolina. This life continued with Jim Crow laws of segregation that dominated the south and influenced all aspects of black family living following the Civil War.

Segregation was a fact of life in my upbringing. Skin culture that has its own rules in terms of racial relationships determined that I be subjected to all the skin color rules of being African American. I became conscious of being black in a subtle, gentle, evolutionary process that first meant being embraced by my immediate and extended family. By the time I became old enough to travel with my mother "across" town to the white side, my identity as black was established and understood within the protective custody of my parents and grandparents. The racism of my hometown was a fact, and I had received an early protective wall from it within my family. By the time of increased encounters with whites at the age of 12, my identifiable value as a human being had become a part of my psyche. My only childhood contact with whites was generally in two locations. One was through my Catholic grammar school where a white man resided as a parish priest. The second was through contact at the neighboring Ford store owned and managed by whites. Their store sat on the racially divided border of Merriman Road, broadly separating the African Americans and white homes in the town. My playmates were all black from my neighborhood or my segregated Catholic school. I did not develop any games that involved a white "Other." Traditional games of marble, jump rope and dolls were all done within my cultural context. There was no reference to a white "Other"—whether negative or positive within these very early years of my childhood.

My African American grammar school nuns, who became my first teachers at age 6, taught me the culturally positive side of being black. Theirs, like my immediate family, was a strong psychological protective stand against the Jim Crow racism of my town.

Co-author Helen and I come together as individuals who have reviewed the work of the other and have found a common meeting space for discussions, wonderment and concern. In this space of the psychological, phenomenological and political, we explore both conscious and unconscious areas of understanding racial relationships. This can be through a changeable lens of depth psychology, traditional healing practice, feminism or current events.

My training as a Jungian analyst never involved any formal discussions regarding racialized language or racism in Jung's writing or theoretical concepts. As I raised my voice in training classes, questioning these things, I was discouraged by teachers to do so. Jung was "a man of his times," and this was to resolve all of the negative ideas he had written or spoken of regarding people of Africanist descent. Apparently, Helen received the same message in her training to become a Jungian analyst. Our relatedness as psychoanalysts supports us in taking the individual, as well as the shared view, through a psychological and political lens that has not been peered through in terms of Analytical Psychology.

One of our challenges as well as our hope is to dig deeply into our own personal unconscious—exploring shadow, so that we might be less afraid of the darkness inherent in the shadow, less afraid of asking the difficult questions that remain hidden behind and within racial and cultural complexes. There are questions and discoveries we will probably dread to see as well as have the desire to uncover. Some of this desire is motivated by our being depth psychologists. Our psychological work is in looking for that which might be in the "underbrush" of the unconscious, hidden as a racial complex with all of its associations and emotionality.

Poet/essayist Audre Lorde has addressed in her writings the ideals of the feminist, political writer and mother. The language of resistance to racism and homophobia flowed through Lorde's work. She spoke what many of Africanist generations understood—*you're silence will not protect you*. The significance of our co-authored book is not only because we engage with one another in a dialogue—it is rather because we wish to discuss aspects of Jungian psychology from two perspectives of differing ethnicities, examining theories and concepts developed in the 19th century at the beginning period of modern psychology. As co-authors, we attempt to decipher the inherent racism that was built into modern European psychology, specifically Analytical Psychology, in its formative years. We believe that this conversation can be heightened, influenced and enriched by the ancestral lineages from which we have evolved. The Africanist experience of the African Holocaust and the "vision of whiteness" created by Europeans predicted centuries of horror for millions. This vision of whiteness can also be seen as holding the pain of white cultural denial for all those who "controlled" the power of the seas, the ships and the enslaved.

As co-authors, Helen and I consider ourselves within a frame not only as "Other"; we are face-to-face with considerations of how we can also be true reflections of one another. We are required to see into projections that make us different and yet can keep us the same. These I believe are a part of our *bonds*. We are tied together not just by our humanity—as members of one race, but also by our willingness to be related in ways of the heart as well as the mind.

Words such as *cultural change initiator* and *citizen therapist* come to mind when I engage in this writing. Analytical Psychology may have emerged from Jung's own investigations into the unconscious and also ego psychology, but his apparent consistent thrust always appeared to be in the direction of individuation (this concept also leaves room for exploration), and toward a return to the collective, to society in the giving of what all the isolated inner work had found. What was the inner found treasure that was to be shared? One of my main questions as a depth psychologist is how can I change consciousness moving from the psychological interior space into the outer place of community, the collective?

Politics matters and gives meaning to my work with individuals and groups as well as the entirety of my life. I do not consider myself to be separate from the issues facing Africanist people as a cultural group or the issues facing me as a member of our collective world. What purpose does it serve to do the psychological work of what Jung has called individuation if nothing emerges that can positively influence a world that is in crisis on so many different levels?

Audre Lorde (2018) says the following in *The Master's Tools Will Never Dismantle the Master's House*:

Over and over again in the 1960's I was asked to justify my existence and my work, because I was a woman, because I was a lesbian, because I was not a separatist, because some piece of me was not acceptable. Not because of my work but because of my identity. I had to learn to hold on to all the parts of me that served me, in spite of the pressure to express only one to the exclusion of all others.

(p.49)

Significant issues might involve a loss of natural resources on a national scale for some countries. For example, recently South Africa was rationing water to its citizens. We have seen how tornadoes and hurricanes ravage parts of the American mid-West and southern states.

Acts of racism are often tied to economics that are in turn tied to poverty and a suppression of civil and human liberties. The racism that showed itself with the Katrina storm and most recently the treatment of Puerto Rican citizens following the Hurricane Maria in the fall of 2017 are explicit examples of a perfect storm of racism, politics and ecology. How can I consider freeing the spirit, mind, emotional body of someone who comes to see me in psychological suffering, without considering the world in which they are cultured and have lived in all of their lives?

The responsibility of the psychoanalyst includes having an awareness of the political collective and what causes harm and potential relief for the patient. Individuals who have been marginalized by society deserve more than only a therapy that seeks to enliven them within the context of the psychoanalytical frame. Should they not be prepared to *see* with full vision all that is possible in the world beyond the analytical room? In a Eurocentric model of psychoanalysis, how best can space be created for the cultural transgenerational suffering of black people? Is this possible?

Analytical Psychology failed in its' initial approach to meeting the multiculturalism aspect of the American population. This multiculturalism demands the viewing of a social landscape that acknowledges racism, racist policies and institutionally racist structures. I think that the ethical work of the analyst is to allow for the patient's cultural world to be brought "into the room." One is always acting out of the culture and political world into which one was born and came of age.

How can I best address the issues embedded in culture that may never have been discussed with a patient—white or black, in terms of psychology and politics? A part of the work is ego strengthening. Am I helping patients with psychological growth by ignoring the complexities of a lived life that includes ethnicity, racism and racial complexes—both individual and collective, national and global? More often now, we confront and are confronted by the history of the *politics of racism*.

My co-authorship with Helen presupposes that we will have differences as well as those things of which we think and agree with, seeking more deepening of ideas and emotions, without abandoning our writing. This writing is an opportunity to share space, time and development of consciousness with another with regard to a mutual and exclusive cultural history. Together and apart, we think about the shaping of who we are as psychoanalysts and women. The writing we do considers Analytical Psychology, *its* culture as well as our own within the context of ethnicity and racism. It is our hope that through the writing of *Racial Legacies: Jung, Politics and Culture*, we create a narrative story that gives a deeply scrutinized historical backward view on race-politics-psychology, as well as a forward faithfully spirited look to the future.

HELEN MORGAN

The suggestion that Fanny and I might write a book together raised intrigue and anxiety in me in equal measures. I had long admired her work, but we had had only minimal contact over the years and have met just once at a conference in London in 2018. We have in common that we are both women and Jungian analysts and we have both been writing on this subject for some years now. But the differences are substantial, and our challenge is how to negotiate a dialogue across those differences as well as across the Atlantic. The scope for misunderstanding between us is considerable. I am fearful of "getting it wrong," of saying something hurtful or exposing something shameful in me. I could be overcontrolling as white people often are or become obsequious from a need to avoid shame and guilt. I recognize that the responsibilities we each have for this project may not be identical and it will require a delicate form of openness if we are to navigate our way through it.

And yet, despite, perhaps because of, all the difficulties of dialogue across the color divide, it seems so important that we try.

I am often asked why I, a white woman, concern myself with the matter of racism. I imagine that's not a question often put to black friends and colleagues when they write and speak on the subject. It will be assumed that it is an aspect of their lived experience so they have no choice but to be conscious of the reality of racism in both its extreme forms and in the more subtle microaggressions that occur on a daily basis. My whiteness brings with it the option to ignore the subject except as an abstract phenomenon that exists elsewhere—regrettable but not really my problem. This light-hued skin I have inherited comes with a blindfold, a free ticket, a permit to ignore the matter altogether. I am considered "White" and therefore a person of no color.

I was born and brought up in Bristol, a city on the West coast of England, about 120 miles from London. It's a wealthy metropolis which, along with Liverpool, Glasgow and London, was one of the most important ports in the British trans-Atlantic slave trade and hence prospered greatly from the profits from that trade. As a response to postwar labor shortages in the United Kingdom, residents of the British colonies were invited to come to the country to work, and many arrived between 1948 and 1971 from the Caribbean. These people are known as "the Windrush generation" in reference to the ship MV Empire Windrush, which arrived in the United Kingdom in 1948, bringing workers from islands such as Jamaica, Barbados, Trinidad and Tobago. Along with the unfamiliar cold and wet climate of Britain, they had to cope with hostility and racism from much of the white British population who were unused to living alongside black people in such numbers. Signs went up in shops and boarding houses saying: "No dogs, No blacks, No Irish." In 1968, the Race Relations Bill, which would make it illegal to discriminate on the basis of color or creed when engaged in commercial services, was making its way through the Parliament. This prompted Enoch Powell, a Conservative MP, to make a speech that strongly criticized mass immigration, with the now famous quote: "... as I look ahead, I am filled with foreboding; like the Roman, I seem to see 'the River Tiber foaming with much blood.'" This "rivers of blood" speech caused a political storm leading to Powell being sacked from the party and marches of both support and opposition throughout the country.

Many of the new arrivals came to live in Bristol, mainly confined to the inner-city area of St Pauls. I lived in the suburbs of Bristol and my school was almost entirely white, so I rarely came across black people in any significant way. If asked to define who I was, I would not have even considered including whiteness as an element of my identity. I understood that I and my family, friends and fellow schoolmates were just the norm.

At school, I learnt about the British Empire with the United Kingdom placed firmly in the center of a map where many exotic lands were colored pink. Bristol's history was explored to some extent and the subject of slavery raised and discussed but almost as an anomaly, an unfortunate but necessary biproduct that came with the "benefits" of British rule for the colonized nations. Our lessons on Wilberforce and the abolition of the trade meant a focus on my white British ancestors as heroes, which subtly managed to mask and even reverse any systematic exploitation on the part of those who operated the trans-Atlantic slave trade for over three centuries beforehand. I attended a Catholic convent school and, taught in part by nuns, we learnt of the work of the missionaries and collected charitable pennies for the "poor" African babies. The only naked people I ever saw were those from African tribes performing strange and exotic rituals in magazines like the National Geographic or at the cinema. Africans were to be patronized or giggled over and, warned by our parents about certain parts of town, black people living here were to be feared. I recall the childhood game we played as we walked along the pavement. If you stepped on a crack, you would be either eaten by a bear or marry a black man. I wasn't sure which was meant to be worse!

This was the 1950s, and change was on the way. British colonial countries fought for their independence and the Empire evolved into the Commonwealth. At home, wider liberations of the 1960s brought at least the notion of equality and respect, and the soundtrack to our adolescent years was the music of Tamla, Motown and Reggae. In the early 1970s, I left university and, for family reasons, returned to Bristol and worked as a teacher in a large secondary school that was in a white working-class estate on a neglected edge of the city where children were bussed in from St Pauls so that roughly two thirds were white and a third were black. Having grown up in a middle-class suburb of the city, both St Pauls and the school area were unknown to me and I found myself having to manage complex and entirely unfamiliar tensions and conflicts between these different groups of school children. Suddenly, I was confronted with a whole set of cultures and assumptions of which I had previously only a vague awareness, and I was struck by just how sheltered and ignorant I had been.

I learnt a huge amount during these three years and greatly enjoyed the work, but my urge to travel and see the world became too pressing, and with two friends I set out on the 70s "Hippy Trail" overland to the Far East. We were away for about 15 months travelling on public transport through countries and cultures as diverse as Iran, India, Afghanistan, Indonesia and Japan where we worked for a while. This was before the days of mobile phones and social media, so we were out of contact with friends and family at home for weeks at a time. It wasn't always easy, especially as three young women adjusting to very different ways that white people and women are viewed in this world and facing constant challenges to assumptions we hadn't even realized were so embedded within us. Stopping a while within cultures that were so very different from our own shifted any implicitly held notion that ours was the "norm." As the distance from home grew, so did our realization that the religious, cultural, political and intersubjective ways of being that we had taken for granted were just that, one way of being among many, many others.

Having returned to the United Kingdom, I worked in therapeutic communities—first with adolescent boys in the West country and later with adults with mental health difficulties in London. This was my first real experience of working with and alongside black clients and colleagues. At the same time, I was training to become a Jungian analyst. Very early on, I came across some of Jung's writing on women and my feminist soul rebelled. I could not accept his pronouncements on the "feminine," the "anima" and, even more so, the "animus." I had to decide how much I would put aside such objections in order that I could continue with the training. I know well the "man of his time" argument—I have used it on myself many times. It's a perspective with some validity, but I learnt that there is a price to pay internally when one is required to swallow the indigestible as a part of the greater meal.

But it was some years later when I read Farhad Dalal's paper "Jung a Racist" that I came to reexamine some of Jung's writings on the so-called "primitive." I was shocked by the realization that I must have read the passages Dalal was quoting during my training but had failed to even register them or their implications. I was beginning to see aspects of my own racism and noticed that this never had arisen in my training analysis. Once again, I wondered at my seemingly endless capacity for denial.

It was when I started to work with a black woman who was in intensive analysis with me that I began to put these experiences together and to think and write about the presence and impact of racism in the analytic encounter. I learnt much from this patient, who I call Dee in the papers that were based in our work together: "Between Fear and Blindness" and "Exploring Racism." The exploration was rooted in long-held political and social concern as well as an interest in the individual psyche—not least my own—two major strands that had woven their threads throughout my life. It was the overlap, the interrelation between our "internal" and "external" worlds that interested me, a relationship that had been articulated in the early 70s through the mantra of the feminist movement: "the personal is political."

The consulting room provides a privileged setting where there is space and time for thoughts, feelings and interactions to emerge and become available for examination. I began to recognize that some could be seen as countertransference, whereas others might be better described as pretransference. These included attitudes, both conscious and unconscious, that we both brought to the encounter due to our different positions regarding the power relations that are created by racism. Exploring the thoughts that emerged in my mind, I started to notice those that were troubling as they seemed to interrupt a sense of myself as basically "good." My feelings of guilt, shame and the fear of "getting it wrong" had to be acknowledged internally so that I stayed within the analytic frame and resisted the urge to avoid the problem of racism and retreat instead to a state of disavowal.

This disavowal I saw reflected in my professional community. Why aren't we more shocked that a profession concerned with the troubled psyche of 21st century Britain has within it so few members from minority ethnic groups? Why do we go so silent on the matter as if there was no problem to address instead of making every effort to examine ourselves, our trainings and our institutions to find the cause of this anomaly? We are, of course, not the only profession to avoid the matter. It is an aspect of what Robin DiAngelo terms "White Fragility," a subtle but formidable defense system that includes a blindness to the very existence of the underlying ideology and our privilege that results from it, thus ensuring its continuation. Consequently, we are unused to engaging in ordinary conversations among ourselves about the fact of that privilege and its implications. We have nothing like the resilience of black friends and colleagues with whom honest engagement becomes fraught with our anxiety, defensiveness and denial. This way, we have to give up nothing and make no real changes so we can keep holding on to what we have. However, I suggest that this comes with a price and it is one that is paid by the psyche.

Samuels defines individuation as "… a movement towards wholeness by means of an integration of conscious and unconscious parts of the personality. This involves personal and emotional conflict resulting in differentiation from general conscious attitudes and from the collective unconscious" (Samuels 1985, p.102). In her book on African Americans and Jungian psychology, Fanny points out that "Jung says that Africanist people are, for the most part, unable to individuate. He says that we do not have the level of consciousness necessary for such a feat" (Brewster 2017, p.43). Besides wondering what impact such a notion might have on a black individual reading Jung's writing, my own experience has led me to believe that this assumption could be turned on its head.

When it comes to the racism of historic and the modern times, white people's choice to stay blind, deaf and silent concerning our own privilege and its impact on the black "other" means that we are opting to remain unconscious of a crucial aspect of our lives and of our selves.

Introduction 11

Thus, it could be argued that it is we who do not have "the level of consciousness necessary" for the feat of individuation. We know that such an achievement requires the hard and endless toil of engaging with and integrating the shadow aspects of ourselves, but if aspects of that shadow are whitewashed out of view, what richness, what potential, what depth might we be missing?

My answer, then, to enquiries about my motivation for interesting myself in this subject is that it is neither altruistic nor, I believe, neurotic, but comes from my concern with my own path of individuation. I encourage those reading this book who are identified as "white" to do so from a similar concern.

"Whiteness" is an emergent, constructed concept that shifts over time and location. Like "Blackness," it is proved to have no biological reality, and yet these terms, this division holds a deep and immense power to shape our social environment. The above brief history is a personal one unique to me and other white people reading this will have had very different histories depending on age, ancestry, ethnicity, geography etc. It is true that in most Western societies like Britain and the United States, the very worst forms of explicit, extreme racism have been legislated against and manifest mainly in those on the far right. This makes it even more possible for the white "liberal" to assume that we have gone beyond racism and ignore the issue. We can project our own racism into racist groups such as the KKK or the English Defence League and retreat into forms of disavowal. If only we had the resilience for more open conversations with black friends and colleagues about their experience of living in this "liberal" world of ours, we might have to think again.

DiAngelo begins her book with a quote from "Killers of the Dream" by Lillian Smith: "These ceremonials in honor of white supremacy performed from babyhood, slip from the conscious mind down deep into muscles ... and become difficult to tear out." Whatever our personal history, wherever we were born, however young or old we are, if we are regarded as "white" we have inherited layers of privilege and supremacy from which we benefit greatly. Because we are not taught to see ourselves in racial terms, we tend to react against the notion of "Whiteness" and seek ways to exempt ourselves from the category through exceptionalism. DiAngelo (2018) in her book *White Fragility: Why It's So Hard for White People to Talk About Racism* challenges such endeavors and suggests that

> Setting aside your sense of uniqueness is a critical skill that will allow you to see the big picture of the society in which we live;

individualism will not. For now, try to let go of your individual narrative and grapple with the collective messages we all receive as members of a larger shared culture. Work to see how these messages have shaped your life, rather than use some aspect of your story to excuse yourself from their impact.

(p.13)

Racial Legacies: Jung, Politics and Culture opens in Chapter 1 with a consideration of Africa and Europe before the beginning of the trans-Atlantic slave trade. While much is documented about European life before the 17th century, the richness and strength of African societies and kingdoms is less familiar to those of us whose education has come from a western perspective. This imbalance is noted and addressed in this chapter with illustrations from African history provided. The acceptance of slavery throughout European history is explored along with the development of color racism and the development of the trade among Africans to work on the plantations in the Americas.

The very different yet intertwined ancestral legacies of the authors in relation to the African Holocaust are laid out and investigated in Chapter 2. Connecting to the African tradition of honoring the links across generations, the psychological implications for those who are descendants of ancestors brought forcibly from Africa to work on the plantations are highlighted. The ancestral legacy for those who descend from the slaves has also to be faced and, while British life went on a long way from the trade itself, the whole society was involved and the country largely built on the profits of the trade. Both authors argue that these inheritances must be faced and mourned by both black and white if we are to move to a fairer, healthier society. In the absence of this work, "whiteness" continues to maintain its privilege through "white ignorance" and the mechanisms of disavowal.

In Chapter 3, it is argued that these are aspects of the racial complex as it operates in the white liberal. Two case examples are used to illustrate how this works. The idea of the transference in both the clinical and the cultural context is taken up to examine how it is affected by the racial complex. Noting how Jungian psychology has a European racial bias, its tendency toward *othering* is challenged with a particular consideration of what this might mean for those who are of African heritage.

This theme is developed in Chapter 4 where the prejudicial bias at the roots of Jung's Euro-centric perspective that excluded African people and others as "lesser" or "primitive" is highlighted. By doing so, Jung failed to learn from an Africanist perspective that also honored the life of the dream. Examples from African mythology are offered to illustrate this point. The racism that lies deep within Freudian and Jungian theory is developed further in the second part of the chapter. Its roots in the racial hierarchies of 19th-century anthropology have implications for Analytical Psychology today, and a plea is made for modern-day Jungian analysts to face these biases and investigate the foundations of certain aspects of our theory.

In Chapter 5, the death of George Floyd in Minneapolis in May 2020 is discussed from two perspectives. One considers what might be learned by white liberals from the tragic event linking what happened with the fact of white privilege and DiAngelo's concept of "white fragility." It is stressed that such learning is essential if white people are to develop the consciousness and capacity necessary to engage in conversations with black friends and colleagues without repeating harm. By way of contrast, the fact of black resilience as demonstrated by the young African American woman Darnella Frazier who persisted in filming the event is noted. This theme is developed in relation to the black and brown bodies that were exploited for economic purposes over centuries by white slavers and were required to be strong and resilient to work on the plantations. The images of the rope, the whip and the gun are put forward as symbols of white power in America, symbols that are denied through the process of whitewashing.

Chapter 6, the "Politics of Race," begins with a dream used as a lens to contemplate the impact of western white supremacy on other indigenous populations and the natural world through colonization, slavery and capitalism. As a leading European power, Britain has been a major player in this process of destruction but fails to face its role and its impact at a collective as well as an individual level. While Britain was a key driver in the trans-Atlantic slave trade, its geographical location far from the shores of the African continent or the plantations of the Americas meant that it was able to profit immensely from the trade while maintaining a sense of righteous distance. In America, slavery and its aftermath were part of daily life, and the chapter focuses on the legal structures in America from 1661 when the Virginia Assembly legally required African slaves to remain enslaved for life through to the Jim Crow laws and the recent moves in Republican states to restrict voting rights following the period of Donald Trump's presidency. The point is that those racist laws are only dismantled through political action and protest and constant vigilance.

"Race" is a fabricated category and a false narrative that divides human beings. It is a construct across which the two authors attempt their dialogue, and in Chapter 7, each ponders their experience of doing so. The fact of color means that each is located differently in the power relations of race, and this impacts both the emotional and the bodily experience of each. Both authors ponder on the experience of maintaining the conversation across the divide throughout the process of working on the book together.

References

Brewster, F. (2017). *African Americans and Jungian Psychology: Leaving the Shadows*. London: Routledge.

DiAngelo, R. (2018). *White Fragility: Why It's So Hard for White People to Talk About Racism*. London: Penguin Random House.

Lorde, A. (2018). *The Master's Tools Will Never Dismantle the Master's House*. London: Penguin Random House.

Samuels, A. (1985). *Jung and the Post-Jungians*. London: Routledge & Kegan Paul.

1 Before the African Holocaust

Africa of Antiquity

The entire African continent, though divided into individual countries, has always had a mutuality of interests, culture and philosophies that can provide a perspective of unity. This idea of unity can be equal to that of any other continent in our world, including Europe. The connectedness of countries within the African continent can be thought of as unified in a historic and life-affirming manner. I emphasize this because there can be a tendency, part of our historical, educational and psychological conditioning, to divide Africa into parts. This was the European colonization of Africa. This came centuries later in the 17th century. Prior to this division, countries on the African continent had geographical differences due to climate, land usage and activities based on the qualities of the land on which the people resided. However, this did not exclude the commonality of cultural traits that belonged to all African people, throughout the continent.

The period of time in African history from the 10th through the 13th centuries was of African richness, development and adherence to political, societal and religious norms of an early people. In research of African history, several African countries have been found to be leaders in the development of various African societies. One of the most important was the ancient country of Ghana that initially existed in the area of the Sudan. In *The Royal Kingdoms of Ghana, Mali and Songhay: Life in Medieval Africa*, authors Patricia and Fredrick McKissack (1994) say the following:

> For countless generations, people have lived in the Sudan, the fertile strip of land just below the Sahara Desert that stretches from the Red Sea on the east to the Atlantic Ocean on the west. They have cleared the land, built their homes, and farmed the savanna,

DOI: 10.4324/9781003025689-2

where six-to seven-feet high elephant grass sways in the hot, dusty breezes. Once they hunted water buffalo, wild hogs, and antelope. They harvested wood from the mahogany, *obechem*, and sapele trees that grew there, and crafted exquisite pieces. They mined gold and iron ore and shaped it into tools and weapons. They traded gold, copper, and salt in cosmopolitan cities such as Timbuktu, Jenne, and Gao, and scholars studied and worshiped at mosques designed by famous architects. They sailed along slow-moving rivers, where venerable crocodiles watched and waited in solemn silence. And children gathered to hear the village storyteller teach them important lessons through stories about snakes, leopards, monkeys, and hyenas. The Arabs called the land Bilad al-Sudan, which means "Land of the Blacks."

(p.xvii)

My remembrance of history lessons that taught me about Africa was very different from the words used by the above authors. Those books were not yet written that could describe the beauty, power and correct history of the African continent. The one exception was Egypt because it had been designated by white archeologists and historians as not being "black." It was noted as having been too advanced to belong to "black Africa." The question and disagreement of whether Egypt was actually "black" has continued for decades. In *Intellectual Traditions of Pre-Colonial Africa*, Constance B. Hilliard (1998) says,

While Eurocentric scholars have traditionally asserted that the ancient Egyptians were "white," their Afrocentric counterparts now insist that this remarkable civilization was "black." While this debate remains ongoing, we should remember that the racial categories of "white" and "black" are not biological. Rather, they represent social constructs peculiar to America and certain other societies.

(p.6)

Continuing, Hilliard (1998) adds, "As for the ancient Egyptians, they appear to have possessed the same diverse hues of skin colors as do their modern-day counterparts. As to whether they were 'Africans,' our contemporary understanding is quite solid that indeed they were." The consistent pattern of separation, segregation and creation of division along ethnic lines, though probably an archetypal pattern, does lend to dividing groups as a defining principle of "whiteness." Separating Egypt from the rest of Africa and claiming it as part of the "white" collective allowed white historians and others to create a designation of the "Dark Continent" and keep Egypt, with its abundance in knowledge, culture and economic richness, for whites. Ghana as an early African kingdom had its own richness of culture. Among these was the formulation and construction of government ran by a kingship, nobles of the court and individuals who served the king. Our modern-day information regarding the structure of Ghana's early medieval society came originally from three different sources. The first was from the oral tradition began and carried for generations by *griots*. These men were present in the villages as well as in the dwellings of the kings. It was because of the memory and storytelling ability of the griot that lines of succession could be determined and maintained. Due to their abilities, it is believed that warriors and kings could be encouraged to fight and win battles when they were facing defeat. Author of *Precolonial Black Africa*, Cheikh Anta Diop (1987) says the following:

> The king was surrounded by a very large body of guards in which the sons of vassal princes served side by side with other members of the nobility. Within this army, in which a lordly, aristocratic mentality reigned, the role of the griot assumed all its sociological significance. Through his songs, which were living accounts of the history of the country in general and the families whose members he addressed, he helped, he even forced the indecisive, fearful warrior to act bravely and the brave to act like heroes, to perform miracles. His contribution to victory was very important: his bravery and often temerity were beyond question, for he too was as exposed to danger as the warriors whose exploits he celebrated; even at the height of the battle, they needed to hear his exhortations which boosted their morale. The griots, then, were not superfluous beings; their usefulness was obvious: they had a "Homeric" social function to fulfill.
>
> (p.120)

The second source of information regarding the early centuries of life in Ghana came through the writings of individuals who recorded the activities of the village people as well as the activities of those who held bureaucratic and leadership positions in the society. These early scribes appeared to have been men from outside the villages and kingships about which they wrote. Two of the most prolific writers of the time, Al Bakri and Ibn Khaldun, are tenth- and 11th-century writers who not only wrote the stories from griots but also chronicled from their own observations. Eventually, with the passage of time and the spread of literacy, more was written about the history of Ghana and other early African kingdoms.

In the years from 500 BC, the Iron Age, through medieval times, the people of Ghana had a highly structured government run by a continuous rulership of kings. The king lived among his citizens in close quarters from where he would emerge and travel among individuals asking about their problems and seeking to solve them through assumed wisdom gained by his status as king. Individuals who succeeded to the throne did so through the matriarchal line of inheritance. This continued through centuries and had a stabilizing effect on the lives of citizens whether in villages or cities. In addition, the prosperity of Ghana was determined by its natural resources. Al Bakri, another recorder of Ghana's ancient history, says the following:

> When (the king) gives audience to his people, to listen to their complaints and set them to rights, he sits in a pavilion around which stand his horses caparisoned in cloth of gold; behind him stand ten pages holding shields and gold-mounted swords; and on his right hand are the sons of the princes of his empire, splendidly clad and with gold plaited into their hair. The governor of the city is seated on the ground in front of the king, and all around him are his viziers in the same position. The gate of the chamber is guarded by dogs of an excellent breed, who never leave the king's seat; they wear collars of gold and silver.
> (p.21)

The people who made up the societies of Ghana were fortunate in their lives due to the wealth afforded to them by the abundance of iron and gold that existed in the caves of their country. The successful usage of iron in creating instruments of war provided Ghanaians with superior weapons to overcome embattled enemies. The prosperity of the country was also achieved by the work of blacksmiths who provided farming tools that allowed agriculture to grow and develop. The country was safe from attacks for long periods of time due to the strength of the king, metal weaponry and the security felt by the citizens due to an abundance of food and protection.

The religion of Africa's Ghana during the period of the Iron Age through the beginning of the tenth century was one of traditional beliefs honoring ancestors, honoring mythological figures such as Ogun, the god of iron and war, and holding to beliefs of both what one could see in the real world and what existed in another invisible world. In the beginning of the eighth century, Islam began to make gains among the

African royal families in the Sudan. Due to the power of the king and the impressive influence he had over his subjects, the conversion of them began slow but increased steadily over the decades. Author Diop (1987) provides three important reasons for the success of Islam in changing religious customs in Ghana. He says,

> The primary reason for the success of Islam in Black Africa, with one exception, consequently stems from the fact that it was propagated peacefully at first by solitary Arabo-Berber travelers to certain Black kings and notables, who then spread it about them to those under their jurisdiction.

The two other reasons for the increase in Islam religious practices were due to holy wars conducted by Black chiefs. Upon conquering villages, members of the community joined him in his faith. Last, Diop notes that there was a "metaphysical relationship" between Islam and African religious beliefs.

The influence of "Islamization" in the Sudan held strong through centuries following its initial introduction in the eighth century. It however has been noted that underneath the practices of Islam, many converts continued traditional practices of offering libations, making animal sacrifices as they practiced the teachings of the Koran. The duality of religious integration that survived for these centuries provided another form of consistent stability to Ghana's society. Coupled with political leadership that embraced Islam, the communities of the king followed and provided economic support through taxation. However, the main source of the country's economic independence and power was through its gold mines. In reviewing the political and economic structure of the Sudan during medieval times, it is apparent that the country had great stability, wealth, religious engagement and powerful leadership. Ghana is an example of an African empire that thrived for centuries. A part of the reason for this was the willingness of the leaders of the country to allow for those who disagreed with politics and the king to leave the country without being harmed. This policy supported the development of allegiances rather than warfare. When political fighting occurred, the loser of the contest—someone who was trying to gain the kingship, was exiled from the country. This type of action added to the stability of the country.

Similar to the political strength of Ghana due to consistency in societal ways was the initiation and longevity of art within the Nigerian region of NOK. The terracotta artwork first discovered in the 1950s, from this region of Nigeria, dates back to the African Iron Age. It has been noted that much of the art pieces found have been taken illegally and sold to European and American private collectors. The beauty and value of African art has been displayed in mostly European museums. The masks of Benin and the textiles of any number of African countries attract attention due their long-lived attributes. The period of time expressed through these forms of African art indicates centuries. The quality of African art endures. Some speak of the functionality of the art, the meaningfulness for which it existed, the purpose of service it provided. It was not art for the sake of art but rather for engagement with life. This is certainly seen with mask making and the relationship between this and the dance. Rituals of life made use of objects holding the energy of the people who created the objects as well as the purpose for such creations. In *Masks of Black Africa*, author Ladislas Segy (1976) says:

> Although most African masks and statuary are from the same woodcarving tradition, the masks are entirely different in style because of their different functions. The masks are usually bold because, first of all, they represented mythological, legendary, nonhuman beings, often animals associated with the founders of the tribe. To give expression to these spirit-beings according to the oral tradition, the carver used his imaginative powers to create masks often fantastic in appearance. This boldness, furthermore, was necessary to compensate for the distance of the masked dancer from his audience, who actively participated in the communal festivities. By contrast, masks and statues used in more intimate, private rituals (such as ancestor and magic cults) often leave a more serene expression.
>
> (p.3)

African art has withstood centuries of scrutiny and appraisal from outside the African communities from which they originated. Their value has been increased not so much by the considerations of Africans themselves but rather by those who stole the images and artifacts from Egyptian places of spirituality, to the underground of the Nok and burial grounds. However, it is important to see the continued underlying understanding of the "art" that was always in service of being a contributor to the transcendence and ease of the community in which the art was created. It added to the life of those who created it and was shared by all who saw or engaged with it—from rituals belonging to rites of passage to festivals honoring the king. Molefi Kete Asante (1998), in discussing African art and function, says the following in *The Afrocentric Idea*:

While it is common for neo-Aristotelian rhetoricians to emphasize the observers in the judgment of discourse, Africans highlight the creative process of the artist. To be an observer is to be primarily interested in the product, but to be an artist means that the creation and its function in society are uppermost. Thus the African sees the discourse as the creative manifestation of what is *called to be*. That which is *called to be*, because of the mores and values of the society, becomes the created thing, and the artist, or speaker, satisfies the demands of the society by calling into being that which is functional ... a meaning that is constructed from the social, political, and religious moments in the society's history.

(p.75)

The energy, disposition and value of an African art piece is then valued by an African consciousness that speaks to the longevity and generations of tradition. The idea of value in time is directly related to the philosophical belief of the continuum of life that develops from an ancestral life force, entering physical embodiment and moving once again into a space and time of what has already been and will repeat through the birth of a child. The sequencing of life is respected through an honoring of those who have come before. Within the Yoruba tradition, this tradition is seen in the *odes* of divination. Author Modupe Oduyoye (1972) in *The Vocabulary of Yoruba Religious Discourse* says,

> The Yoruba says that if a man does not know where he is going, at least he should know where he is coming from. When a man is puzzled about the future unknown, he goes to a *babalawo* who knows where things began; and he plots the man's future course for him by tracing his particular situation to ancient precedents. After all, *ko si ohun ti oju o ri ri* (there is nothing which eyes have not seen before).

The African philosophical underpinnings that existed for centuries in ancient and medieval Africans show resiliency in their African Diaspora descendants. The transmission of African music, dance and linguistics brought over by slaves thrived through the African Holocaust. Even within the area of religion—because this was most significant, in the Caribbean and southern United States, the orisha of Yoruba tradition joined with Catholic rituals in a manner not like the initial engagement of Islam and tradition in eighth-century Sudan.

The stories of Africa that we have *not* been told are the ones that we must learn. In looking at present-day diaspora, we can gather ideas regarding how African beliefs and societies thrived for centuries. The political and social climate of life today demands that people of Africanist ancestry must still embrace and develop a perspective that can see into a past of ancestral strength of survival, and look to a future of rebirth and transformation. It is possible to keep re-creating and keeping alive the vision of a positive intergenerational story. This would be one as imagined and told by the griot of ancient Africa who had memory for such a telling. It is in the nature of an African consciousness to hold the past while looking to the future. This is what has ensured the survival of Africanist communities since and beyond the Middle Passage.

EUROPE BEFORE THE TRANS-ATLANTIC SLAVE TRADE

Helen Morgan

The Acceptance of Slavery

Two key questions arise when considering both slavery and racism in Europe prior to the trans-Atlantic slave trade. The first is why there was so little objection to the practice of slavery in either the classical or the Christian European world until the early 19th century. In "The Problem of Slavery as History," Joseph Miller (2012) puts it this way:

> Over more than two millennia of Western history ... slavery had flourished at the very moments most celebrated in the Western tradition of freedom. These paradoxical combinations of slavery and freedom included classical Athens, otherwise known for democracy; the Roman Empire's civilizing of barbarian north western Europe; fifteenth-century Florence at the height of Renaissance humanism; and eventually in the Americas at the very birth of modern civic freedoms. How could these champions of the story of Western progress toward modern human rights not have recognized the obvious need to eliminate the inhumanity of human bondage?
>
> (p.13)

We are looking back at ancestors whose ideologies, ethical codes and morality differed, at least in part from our own. The current concept of human rights is a relatively recent one as, it seems, is the repugnance we feel toward the notion that one human being could consider another his property. Slavery was accepted as a feature of European societies for the larger part of the history of this continent.

It was certainly a substantial feature of the classical world. Greek pride in its democratic, rational system of governance included a disparagement of those societies and cultures that were not Greek. The term *barbarian* comes from the Greek word *barbarous* meaning "babbled" and referred to those who lacked the democratic political language of the Greeks. The enslavement of those conquered in distant "barbaric" lands meant that the Athenian citizens were freed from physical work to engage in the system of democracy for which they were known.

The division of humanity that licensed one group (in this case, the Greeks) to enslave another were supported by the philosophy of the day. Aristotle believed that humanity was split between free men and those who lacked certain capabilities such as the capacity to think properly, and he posited the concept of "natural slavery" as the fitting condition for this latter group.

This view, endorsed by Plato, assumes differences in the very bodies and souls of humans and draws on a comparison with animals. This justification of the practice of slavery within ancient Greek society echoed down the generations and was culturally transmitted through classical education to the ruling classes of the 19th century.

Slavery was rife throughout the Roman Empire, which reached across the entirety of Europe and into Asia. Captured through warfare, thousands of slaves were transported across great distances for use by Roman citizens of the towns. At the height of the Empire, it is reckoned that about one-third of the population of Rome was enslaved.

> Slaves found their way into all corners of the economies and societies in the classical world. Much of the heavy laboring tasks, in agriculture, mining, construction, fell to the slaves. Slaves dominated domestic work and even many skilled occupations. Some were highly trusted, skilled and literate; others were mere brutes of labour or warfare: manning the galleys or acting as gladiators entertaining the crowds in the amphitheaters.
> (Walvin 2007, p.8)

Europe entered the so-called Dark Ages when a loose-knit system of kings and princes replaced the Imperial rule of Rome. Slavery continued in different forms but was gradually eroded by the rise of feudalism and serfdom. Here a system of debt bondage and indentured servitude kept the peasantry tied to the Lord of the Manor for whom they worked. In return, they were entitled to protection, justice and the right to cultivate a proportion of the land for their own subsistence.

Feudalism was the form of government throughout Europe between the 9th and 15th centuries. Around 1347, the bubonic plague—known as the Black Death—arrived in Europe from Asia. One of the most devastating pandemics in human history, it spread rapidly and is estimated to have killed between 30% and 60% of Europe's population. It particularly ravaged the peasantry who had made up about 90% of the population. Whilst monetary payment for labor had already been introduced to a minimal degree, the shortage of peasants, laborers and artisans caused by the plague meant a rapid acceleration of the system of waged labor and the decline of feudalism.

Slavery featured strongly in the continuing conflict between Christians and Muslims in the Mediterranean. Christian Crusades, or "holy wars," continued from the 11th to the 17th century, some involving a fight for the "Holy Land" and some against the Iberian Moors and the Ottoman Empire. Slaves were created throughout and on both sides as part of the spoils of war.

Slavery was mentioned in both the Old and New Testaments and was, on the whole, accepted by the Catholic Church. St. Augustine of Hippo (354–430 CE) considered that:

> The prime cause, then, of slavery is sin, which brings man under the dominion of his fellow ... which does not happen save by the judgement of God, with whom is no unrighteousness, and who knows how to award fit punishments to every variety of offence.
> (St Augustine, The City of God, 2003, 19:15)

He argued that slavery was unknown until "righteous" Noah "branded the sin of his son" with that name (ibid.). This refers to the story in the Old Testament of the Bible (Genesis, 9), which tells how Ham failed to cover his eyes and saw his father, Noah, naked and drunk; as a consequence, God cursed the descendants of Ham and his son Canaan. The curse condemned all future generations of Ham's line to servitude to the children of the other obedient sons. Throughout the history of European trade in slaves from the African continent, this story was a central plank in the argument to justify such activities. For the white masters, considered the descendants of Japheth, the keeping of slaves is validated. Indeed, through being endorsed by God Himself, it becomes almost a duty.

Thomas Aquinas largely agreed with Augustine that slavery was the result of the Fall, but he also argued that the nature of heaven demonstrated that some angels were superior to others and that this hierarchical structure was mirrored on earth giving some men a natural authority over others. It wasn't really until the mid-18th century that any substantial Christian movement decrying the very existence of slavery established any momentum through the development of the Quaker movement.

The Rise of Color Racism

This brings me to my second question, which concerns the rise of color racism and its division of humanity between "black" and "white."

Africans were known to live in Britain during Roman times not only as soldiers or slaves but also as free men and women. According to Miranda Kaufmann (2017), author of "Black Tudors: The Untold Story", by Tudor times black people were present in small numbers in the royal courts from Henry VII to James I and lived and worked at many levels of society. They were acknowledged as citizens and, importantly, were being baptized and married and buried in the church. Tudor England before the involvement in the slave trade was:

> an island nation on the edge of Europe with not much power, a struggling Protestant nation in perpetual danger of being invaded by Spain and being wiped out ... The English colonial project only really gets going in the middle of the 17th century. She then asks the important question: How did we go from this period of relative acceptance to become the biggest slave traders out there?
> (Guardian interview, by Bidisha, Oct 29, 2019)

At the time of the great maritime expansion of the 15th century, European states were monarchical and aristocratic, and governments ruled through traditional loyalties and imperial links where they had territories abroad. Until this point, trade had largely been within Europe itself and around the Mediterranean, but during the 15th and 16th centuries, it became apparent that conquest and trade in territories further afield brought wealth that would greatly enhance political power at home.

At first, the search was for goods such as gold rather than slaves. The need to outflank the Islamic world and reach the Asian markets by going around Africa led to the discovery of lucrative territories. The Portuguese were the main players in these early explorations:

> In the 1439s and 1440s, successive voyages pressed further south along the African coast, at each point touching on internal African trade routes which yielded goods (and humanity) from deep inside

Africa. The early slaves taken to Portugal were Arab, Berber and black African. In 1444 the first batch were displayed in a field outside Lagos in southern Portugal.

(Walvin 2007, p.37)

Both Portugal and Spain colonized the islands of the Canaries and Cape Verde where cane sugar was grown. Sugar had been known in Europe but mainly in the countries of the Eastern Mediterranean. There seemed an unlimited appetite for this sweet substance in Europe, and new territories were needed to grow this highly profitable crop. African slaves were brought in to work on these plantations, and the link was gradually established between sugar cultivation and African slave labor.

The British entered the trade in 1562 when John Hawkyns sailed from England, captured several hundred Africans off the coast of Sierra Leone and took them to what is now known as the Dominican Republic. He returned with a cargo of ivory, hides and sugar. Back in London, Queen Elizabeth stated: "(i)f any African were carried away without their free consent it would be detestable and would call down vengeance from heaven upon the undertakers" (Hazlewood 2004, p.91). It seems, however, that this moral outrage, this initial, instinctive, human revulsion was soon quelled when she came to realize the extent of the profits to be made. Instead, she provided Hawkyns with a ship, which came to be known as "The Good Ship Jesus" and sent him back to Africa with her royal blessing. Thus began the British involvement in and eventual domination of this terrible business.

Europe was deeply divided with periodic wars between nations and rivalries that lasted centuries. Nevertheless, Europe seemed united in the commitment not to use other Europeans as slaves. Europeans were prepared to settle new territories with indentured labor, shipping vagrants, convicts and prisoners of war to the new settlements in their thousands. However, they remained free men and women.

Prior to the use of enslaved Africans, slaves could be black, white, Christian, Muslin or pagan. Despite the fact that there had been significant Arab trading previously with Black Africa, there was virtually no link between slavery and Blackness until maritime Europeans engaged in the form of chattel slavery. This meant that slaves began to be marked as of a different, darker skin color. In the Americas, to prevent the indentured European laborers from aligning with the Africans, a system of laws privileging white people developed consolidating the division of "black" and "white" emerging in the Western mind.

Once the idea of the "races" was established with the black regarded as "primitive" and the white "civilized," there could develop a justification of colonization and slavery of the former by the latter. Celia Brickman (2018) considers this at length in her book "Race and Psychoanalysis." She says:

> When Columbus set sail for the Indies and found himself instead in the New Worlds, already in place were two distinct frameworks for comprehending outsiders. The first was a medieval literary and popular discourse about outsiders as barbarians, wild men and noble savages, while the second was a religious-legal discourse, consolidated during the Crusades, concerning the treatment of infidels and the lawful right of Christians to the confiscation of uninhabited and non-Christian lands.
>
> (pp.19–20)

In Europe, from the start there was profound ambivalence toward these dark-skinned "others." On the one hand, the "Wild Man," linked as he was to the descendants of Ham and the "barbarian," was a frightening but also envied object who could give full rein to his passions unrestrained as he was by "civilized" laws. The "Noble Savage," on the other hand, was regarded as still living in the Garden of Eden and thus represented a lost paradise of innocence and peace that existed before Europeans were burdened with the demands of civilization. "The contrasting images of the Wild Man and the Noble Savage ... contributed to a contradictory discourse which represented non-Europeans as both idealized and depraved, fulfilled in their simplicity yet lacking in their humanity" (Brickman 2018, p.21).

In this brief summary of certain aspects of European history, one consistent theme that emerges is the capacity of the human mind to *both* hold an ideal of freedom *and* justify the fact of human bondage. Another is the ability of humans to develop a system of racism that constructs a category of people for mercenary purposes, and which regards those who had previously been known and lived alongside as inferior and mere property. Perhaps these paradoxical dynamics within the human psyche need bearing in mind if we are to fully face the racism that continues to saturate our societies.

Dialogue

**TRANSCRIPT OF FANNY/HELEN CONVERSATION
APRIL 20, 2021**

FANNY You know I didn't read your paper again on Europe before the transatlantic slave trade because I wanted to not think about Europe. You see I could talk about Charlemagne and the 100 years war because these sorts of things are in my head automatically, but things about Africa are not. So I thought if I read Helens paper I'm going to be holding Europe in my head again and I tried to avoid holding Africa opposite Europe even though that's kind of our task. I'm really trying to block the European perspective because I don't really know enough about the African perspective to be able to write from that, from that place, so I felt that if I read your piece then I would be deep in European history again. For me it's like the focus needs to be on Africa before colonization because we don't know enough about that and it's hard to know about that.

HELEN It's absolutely true that we have so little knowledge about African history.

FANNY We learned about Europe and European history which was fascinating, but we didn't learn about kingdoms in Africa. Africa had kingdoms and Kings and Queens and so when you read that princes were brought over on slave ships it seemed like crazy talk. How could that be possible? But within those countries, in those years, those centuries they had kingdoms and empires. I intentionally stayed away from slavery in Africa because one of the things that happens is whites will say "Oh, there was slavery in Africa" and then I have to write about how it was not the same as American slavery. It *was* not the slavery that took place in America.

HELEN It was my main note about your piece—the absence of anything on African slavery. The trouble is if you don't put it in it looks like an idealization of Africa and I think it needs acknowledging. I gather that slavery before the trans-Atlantic slave trade took a very different form.

FANNY You see in the beginning it was that slaves were indentured family members and treated like family members, so they became part of the family and eventually they got their freedom. In the beginning it was very similar to the way it was in Europe.

HELEN I absolutely take your point that when people say that there was slavery in Africa too it's usually defensive but I think it needs a mention.

FANNY I could say it, but again I'm coming up against that thing of comparing it to Europe.

HELEN I don't think you need to compare it to European slavery because the other thing that people say (which was true) is that on the whole it was Africans who captured the slaves and sold them to the Europeans. Again, I think it just needs acknowledging or otherwise it reads shadowless.

FANNY I feel like Africa has carried so much shadow. It's the dark continent. I feel I want to be totally in the light with this because I'm tired of it being the dark continent.

Its like you're saying the piece is an idealization of Africa and I'm saying, okay, why not? We've done that with stories from Europe from the beginning, that Africans were just pagans, Europe serfs, and you know feudalism wasn't any great fun for people who didn't have money.

I guess we're looking at Africa before slavery. I'm thinking of Joseph Conrad and "the dark continent." I'm thinking about Africa in that light and my instinct, my impulse is to make it light, to shine the light on it. So how is that working with us as we begin our project of looking at Africa? You're saying "don't idealize it" and I'm saying "I want to."

HELEN The reverse is true for me I can very easily demonize Europe and it was interesting writing this piece as it put it in a context. I can get into that opposite that Europe was all shadow, that everything in Europe was nasty and brutal, which of course is not true either although there were a lot of people suffering in Europe at the time. Either opposite simplifies. It loses the complexities. What has happened to African history from a European point of view it is that it is made it very simple, and all the complexities and richness of the different cultures have been lost.

FANNY I'm arguing a little bit from the opposite point of view. Africa was a continent like Europe. There are groupings of language that show unity and yet we have this consciousness around Africa as divided because of European intervention. But it's just like looking at Europe—Austria, Germany, Czechoslovakia, Russia—like Europe is joined together even though there's this European mindset that wants to divide things. It works in the division of Africa: the Belgians can have this and the French can have that ... It looks like a European mindset which is different from an African mindset -which is that we are one. It doesn't have to be the negative *participation mystique*.

HELEN I was thinking about that film they showed at the CAP conference about the 19th century division of Africa and when you look at the boundaries of some of the countries we just put a ruler to draw straight lines across natural groupings. The complexities of a rich continent were completely ignored. They just divided up the land and the people according to the wishes of the European powers regardless of who was actually living on the land. So many of the wars we've seen in Africa were because of European manipulation.

FANNY I didn't want to go into the 19th century because I wanted to look at Africa before the slave trade. So I had to come to the tip of the 16th century. Modern time began in the 16th century and for Africa it meant the intrusion of the Portuguese bringing in guns in that way starting to change African culture. Even Islam didn't do that.

You talk about Christians and Muslims in conflict in the Mediterranean and I think I'd like to address that. Islam sort of crept into the Sudan and into Africa because of the trading that was happening. I first learned that Islam was this fierce attack on black Africa, but it really wasn't like that.

That might be one of our questions in this section, what kind of lens do I want to use for this African history? This is our narrative text and this is our oral narrative which follows in the oral tradition so we are doing something that has historic roots. In the beginning there were storytellers in every culture. The questions could be over the dialogue that we are now having and then go into the text maybe the questions lead us into what we're writing about and it gives it a frame for it.

HELEN It's also about the lenses we have already inherited. What I learned about Africa as a child was mostly about poverty and starvation. There were terrible pictures on television of starving Biafran children dying. I recall collecting pennies for the poor African babies. It was very condescending and from a British colonial perspective. When I was growing up, we still had an Empire and we had a map at school that was still painted pink which is where all the British colonies were. The only naked people I ever saw were Africans on our Pathe news or in geographical magazines or something. Like it didn't matter that they were naked. And I got a sense of just one monoculture—everyone was the same and everyone always had been the same so there is no development. And how lucky they were that the British had come and brought civilization to them. That's a powerful lens to be given as a child. And black British children were given the same lens.

FANNY That's right that's an important question I think. So one question is "what kind of lens should I use to view Africa?" and now your question is more "what is the inherited childhood lens that has influenced my view of Africa?"

HELEN I assume you must have had something similar?

FANNY Very similar. But people *were* starving in Africa and there was truth to that. But they weren't starving in antiquity. They had agriculture and they had blacksmith's. Something shifted.

HELEN Well our history lessons didn't include the fact that most of the wars and famines that took place had been caused by the arrival of the Europeans and colonialism. It was put down to a failure in the African psyche.

FANNY That's right. It wasn't due to invasion. It wasn't due to an interruption which created arrested development in Africa. Which goes to white guilt about what's happened there.

Which goes to "African kids are starving. We have to give money." That's what happens when you steal the gold and bodies from a country. There's got to be some guilt. There's got to be something that matches that kind of rape of a continent.

HELEN And there is the question of African debt. This idea that most of African countries are considered to be in debt. The debts were huge and there were questions of how were they going to pay it back. I recall the Pan African movement worked out how much Europe owed Africa in gold taken, diamonds taken, people taken, bodies taken, children taken.

> All that was stolen from Africa -and it far outweighs what Africa is considered to owe.
>
> FANNY   Yes Europe owes Africa a huge debt so it's fine if they invest their money in bodies and medicine and technology and all of that into Africa. They should because they owe it to Africa. It's like reparations. So that becomes my perspective on it.

References

Asante, M.K. (1998). *The Afrocentric Idea*. Philadelphia: Temple University Press.

Augustine of Hippo. (2003). *The City of God*. London: Penguin Classics.

Brickman, C. (2018). *Race in Psychoanalysis: Aboriginal Populations in the Mind*. London & New York: Routledge.

Diop, C.A. (1987). *Precolonial Black Africa*. Chicago: Lawrence Hill Books.

Hazlewood, N. (2004). *The Queen's Slave Trader: John Hawkyns, Elizabeth I and the Trafficking in Human Souls*. London & New York: Harper Perennial.

Hilliard, C.B. (Ed.). (1998). *Intellectual Traditions of Pre-Colonial Africa*. Boston: McGraw-Hill.

Kaufmann, M. (2017). *Black Tudors: The Untold Story*. London: Oneworld.

McKissack, P. & McKissack, F. (1994). *The Royal Kingdoms of Ghana, Mali, and Songhay: Life in Medieval Africa*. New York: Henry Holt & Company.

Miller, J.C. (2012). *The Problem of Slavery as History: A Global Approach*. New Haven & London: Yale University Press.

Oduyoye, M. (1972). *The Vocabulary of Yoruba Religious Discourse*. Ibadan: Daystar Press.

Segy, L. (1976). *Masks of Black Africa*. New York: Dover Publications, Inc.

Walvin, J. (2007). *A Short History of Slavery*. London & New York: Penguin Books.

2 Imagining Our Ancestors

Poem

Ogun a da jo
Ogun will be the judge

In the forest
the trees stop echoing the drum
silence sits on our ears
our tongues
for days we listen
our children fuss
our wives prepare more food for Ososi
ask more of our ancestors
increase their prayers to Ogun.

Does he still listen?

Fallen forest leaves lay in silence
prepare for the footsteps of strangers
we know will come
the elders have also fallen silent
those who choose leave
abandon this forest land of our fathers.

We move as branches
swayed by the breath of approaching death
the red sky lowers herself
trees bend
their tops touch the forest floor
bent in sorrow.

By author Fanny Brewster
Unpublished Manuscript/*Journey the Middle Passage: Poems*

Binding Legacy: Ancestor

I imagine my first African ancestor's half-blind gaze as he leaves the slave ship in Charleston, South Carolina. Now, arriving on land, having spent three months in the hold of a ship bearing a name such as *Diligence*. Not unlike the purposefulness of the sacred name of a god—*Mercurio*, which in 1823 took ancestors from West Africa, transporting them to Southeast Brazil. Not unlike the *Madre de Deus* or *The Good Ship Jesus*—the first British slave ship to arrive in America in 1562. These holy names are painted on the ship's bow. The ships have been sent off with the blessings of European monarchies and the Roman papacy, to capture human lives that exist to them only as inhuman African cargo. This is the Middle Passage, a phase of the African Holocaust of which my first ancestor was an unwilling and persecuted victim. The ships holding him, and other captive African men, arrive on the stolen waterways of soon to be enslaved and genocide native indigenous people.

> The Indians were the first occupants of the area surrounding Winyah Bay; the Spaniards probed the region at times; the English finally dominated. The Indians who inhabited what is now South Carolina belonged, according to the ethnologists, to three linguistic stocks: the Iroquoian, the Muskhogean, and the Eastern Siouan.
> (*The History of Georgetown County, South Carolina*, George Rogers, 1985, p.9)

I imagine that my African ancestor is weak. His muscles laying loose next to bones, moving only at the whim of white men crew members who force him to exercise—as they choose. Forced dancing on deck to the crew's shouts and screams, letting the few snippets of air enter his lungs on days when sun sent rays through blue sky. My first stolen Americanist ancestor must have cried as he left the tall trees of his savannah. The mother, father, sisters of his family gone—forever. The village where he had grown to young manhood passing through the rituals of his rites of passage—gone and soon to be replaced with rituals of auctions, clearing swamp land for rice plantations, staring into the future of his enslaved children.

The centuries of time weaving through ancestral life has brought me here today.

As I prepared this writing, I thought about my ancestors—then I thought about my one ancestor, the man or woman who arrived in Charleston, South Carolina, in the 1700s.

Memory

It can be like a soft cocoon, wrapping up centuries of what was *not* passed down in the African American culture. All that was missing in the daily life of African teaching. We know that trauma causes memory loss. How can we expect to recover the memory loss of slave ship torture and plantation life? You might ask why would we want to?

Memory. It was such an essential aspect of African life because it was through this that my ancestor could honor and have a connection to his past as well as his future. His present life was the energetic force that bound the other two ends together. That bound his life—his own ancestors and *his* descendants.

> The doctrine of reincarnation is based on a cyclical trajectory with no beginning and no end, and death as another kind of life. With this orientation, one's sense of time must sit on a different axis from the one on which sits the common Western sense of time, with its discrete, unilinear notion of past, present, and future (Duncan 1998).
>
> (*The Afterlife Is Where We Come From*, Alma Gottlieb, 2004, p.80)

Today, I write, attempting to remember something of what my ancestral lineage is—what binds me to the culture that I now claim as an Africanist. There are physical markers, my skin color being the most dominant. However, there are internal psychic markers that I might call archetypal—the energies that are a part of my ancestral DNA. This is what I bring to my everyday life. It is not always in the most positive of collective or societal ways that I am reminded, or that I remember the lineage of my skin. What it remembers from a racialized American history.

The vague recollections of a deja vu moment where I seem to be not of the 21st century but rather in a broke-down plantation shack or standing on the wooden planks of an 1840s southern pier. I speak and write about these things because they are a part of who I am as a Jungian analyst. My previous clinical training and work as such was not left at the door when I first entered the New York C.G. Jung Institute. I brought myself—as much as I could remember—and all that belongs to my ancestral DNA. I brought the emotional body that had guided me into that brownstone building on East 39th street to begin my psychoanalytical training.

I do believe in the African philosophy that says I am not separated within myself by parts. I am whole within myself and I also belong to others in a continuum. This is the psychological orientation in which I was raised, my heritage, my family, my culture. This also means that my clinical work in the temenos is not separate from who I am as a woman of African descent. During Jung's lifetime as he did his work, and conducted his research, traveling and writing, he brought his culture with him. His culture determined his writing.

It is with love and deep respect that I acknowledge my first *African American* ancestor, though I do not even know his or her name. Though centuries have passed preventing me from claiming his or her name, my African birth name, I can feel, yet understand, through an intuitive sense and know from the relationship with my parents and grandparents, that my ancestor had strength, and that beautiful essence of survival of which Maya Angelou speaks when she says, *and still I rise.*

African Americans and Africans, I wish to call us by the name Africanist, are continuously seeking ways and means of discovering and reverencing our past identities. The problems that accompany these issues confront individuals as well as the communal, cultural group. I realize that these problems of ethnicity are not limited only to our Africanist group.

However, the uniqueness of the African Diaspora is marked by the tragedy of the African Holocaust. The psychology of finding one's self and recognizing lineage and history is crucial in any individual process as well as for the survival of community. The difficult moment arrives in the recollection of how we have come to lose broad sections of the tapestry of our cultural past through the African Holocaust. How to reconcile European influence with Africanist values is an ongoing issue not just for those left in Africa but also for the African Diaspora.

In *Seeking the Sakhu: Foundational Writings for an African Psychology,* author Wade W. Nobles (2006) speaks of Africanist individuals: "The other issue that needs to be discussed is that while we are trying to minimize the destructive forces of white supremacy, we also have to make efforts to maximize the utilization of our cultural systems for human development" (p.265).

The metaphysical manner in which Africanists think of time further supports a claim for the metaphysical nature of African thought. In the Yoruba tradition, one's birth is connected with time in such a way that it is possible to identify one's birthday with a particular god. This in turn provides some direction in determining personality. Then there were those early days of enslavement, when missionaries were inventing and writing the story of *our* consciousness. They began telling our stories instead of the *griots*.

The distortion and denigration of African heritage, our bodies, our culture as first told by the invaders of Africa has carried through to this 21st century. We can see it in many forms of our American society. Time has been very narrow in changing the consciousness with which Africanist people can be viewed by whites, even as American citizens. Time is important because it links one to ancestors and provides some element of prediction of future events. Customs and rituals show respect for elders and ancestors indicating that present time is limited, and must include a wider, more holistic view of life and one that is inclusive of death. When Jung began building his home at Bollingen in Switzerland, he initially thought to use the architectural model of an African hut. Even though he later changed the structure of his building to stone-based more on a European model, the idea of the ancestor continued in his thoughts and his dreams. Jungian psychology as it is practiced has a profound attachment to considerations of the ancestors and how they influence us in contemporary life.

Much of a clinical psychoanalytical practice is based on the significance of paternal and maternal grandparents and great grandparents. We are not only interested in the specific current story of the patient's life but also want to know the narrative of how they came to be the people they are through their ancestors, their cultural inheritance. An Africanist perspective acknowledges that this comes from an ancestral lineage bonding. In traditional healing practices within the Africanist tradition, families are an essential part of the treatment of any individual. This is of benefit to the entire family, not just one individual. The underlying philosophy that guides the work is that one individual does belong to a group and both are almost equally significant. The development of contemporary family systems psychotherapy can testify to the healing potential of a family consciousness in therapeutic practice.

In Africanist consciousness, there is no psychological struggle to preserve the skin, the need for botox. There is no obsession to take care of it in such a way as if it will mean the permanent preservation of the physical body—of life itself. This goes against the philosophical understanding that life continues, whether in the body of a recently passed ancestor or one from a longer period of time. It might seem insignificant to think about the consciousness of how we perceive our skin, but in the narrative of racial relations and racism in the American collective, *skin as culture* has been and continues to be vitally important. From a depth psychological point of view, it is not only the surface that requires attention but also that which lies underneath. In considering the "underneath" of the body and our desire to preserve it or release it through death, there are cultural considerations that are dependent on traditional spiritual and philosophical beliefs. This is an important aspect of what I bring to my clinical work with my patients. As I view the analysand who sits with me, I am open to broadening my conscious self to include this within the phenomenological field. A consciousness of raciality and the politics of racism can exist within this field.

Since Africans held philosophical beliefs regarding the continued existence of the life force energy—intergenerationally, it would follow that the attention is not only given to a singular individuated bodily existence but also includes a perspective that incorporates a view of eternity through the communal, and therefore through ancestors. When I consider the concept of unity between levels of consciousness, it seems reflected in the dreams of my patients as well as in my own dreams. In further consideration of African belief regarding this issue, as individuals and societies become more cognizant of the earth and its resources, an ecological movement has developed that accepts the spirit of everything on the planet and sees the connectedness between all things in existence. The African experience of life and respect for nature in all its aspects continues to be a standard, although until recently an unrecognized and frequently racially maligned, one.

The Akan peoples' theory of "being" is based on the lived experience with a "Supreme Being" at the top. This vertical view of life encompasses God, deities, ancestors, humans and objects of nature from top to bottom. Every aspect of this vertical existence contains sunsum. Kwamu Gyekye (1987) gives a very lengthy, detailed description of sunsum, stating that it is the spirit or quality that exists in all things. As he progresses, Gyekye further details his definition of sunsum as a part of the okra (soul) that is also one's personality. He states that the Akans' concept of a person is dualistic and "interactionist." There is no separation of body and soul as in the Cartesian model because both okra and honam (body) are joined together by the spirit of sunsum that keeps all things together. This is important in considering the healing practices of the Akan community.

Author Wade W. Nobles (2006) says in *Seeking the Sakhu: Foundational Writings for an African Psychology*:

> Traditional African belief systems understand everything in the universe to be endowed with the "Supreme Force." Accordingly, the

nature of existence or being, the ontological conception of the universe, was believed to be Force or Spirit or Power. Because all things were endowed with the same Supreme Force or Power, it was logical to believe that all things are interconnected or interdependent or one.

(p.149)

Individuals in the Akan community believe that they are more likely to be healed by the traditional healer than by the Western practitioner because of their spiritual belief. A sickness in the body is also a reflection of a sickness in the soul. This is an aspect of African philosophy underlining healing practices that traveled and grew in dimension within the African Diaspora.

My first African American ancestor came from the west coast of Africa, at first I believed Guinea.

The family who first bought my ancestor was a South Carolina rice plantation family of British/Scottish extraction. This family, the Wragg(s), had arrived in South Carolina sometime in the early 1700s, settling first in Charleston, South Carolina.

My ancestral family members moved to Georgetown, South Carolina, sometime between 1718 and 1721.

The town of Georgetown was first established in 1703 by a British land grant. This is the town in which my father and grandfather were born. Even today, we have family members who continue to live in both Charleston and Georgetown with the slave surname of Wragg.

My first enslaved ancestor probably arrived in Georgetown by ferry as this was the early means of travel between Charleston and Georgetown during the mid-18th century. The waterways of the area had several rivers, and this was an easy and safest way for transporting goods and African slaves. During the next three decades following the original British throne land grant, Georgetown was divided and sold by land plots, purchased by white settlers who had become the merchants and planters in the geographical area that became known as the low country. Among the early Georgetown settlers was Samuel Wragg Jr., relative of Joseph Wragg of Charleston. This surname is only relevant because it becomes a guiding string that can provide a historical context for gaining information regarding my own ancestral lineage. One of the harshest damages of slavery and an aspect of intergenerational trauma was the loss of original African names and tribe affiliations. Slave owner surnames have then become a possible link to where the families of the African Diaspora survived, lived and created families and extended families during slavery times.

The plantation on which my African ancestor arrived and on which his descendants worked for over a century was primarily the Mansfield plantation on the Black River.

When the Mansfield and Wedgefield plantations were joined through purchase, my ancestor and his relatives worked between both of these plantations. My grandaunt Manda, sister to my grandfather, wrote me a letter 40 years ago describing as much as she could remember about my family line.

Both the Mansfield and Wedgefield plantations were located on the Black River, a few miles north of Georgetown. It is on one of these plantations that my paternal great-great-grandfather, Anthony Wragg was born in 1825. The history of the earlier ancestral years is less clear and requires more historical research.

I understand that my ancestor's enslaved work life began early in the morning and continued until sunset. My ancestors worked on the plantations producing indigo and later rice crops for the white Wragg family. For their labor, they were given a slave shack—some still standing today on the Mansfield plantation, food, and Sundays without having to work in the fields. It appeared that most of my ancestors remained on those two plantations for generations. My ancestors did not live with many other enslaved African people, as the number of slaves on the Mansfield plantation did not appear to be larger than 200 at any given time. Yet even one enslaved ancestor is painful to think about because he represents but one life in what was a holocaust for so many of African descent.

Twelve million Africans are estimated to have died because of the Middle Passage.

It was not uncommon for small to medium plantation owners, with a small number of slaves, to keep families together whenever it was economically convenient for the owner. However, black families could be separated at any time given the economic needs or emotional whims of the slave owner or his wife. This was from the first beginning days of slavery at the auction blocks and continued through until the end of the physical bondage of slavery. In the minds of whites, the bodies of the enslaved belonged to the slaver.

Africans and the descendants had been purchased as part of a production system. Slavery had never existed as a continuous centuries-long economic system with the exploitation of human beings as it developed in the Americas.

My first African ancestor and his descendants' fate as slaves became tied to the descendants of the white Wragg family for over 100 years and remained so through the Emancipation Proclamation in 1865. I believe that my ancestral lineage mothers were midwives and provided health and healing to my early family members as well as to the white Wragg slave owner family. One reason for this was the absence of professional white medical doctors and more important the healing medicine and care of Africans and later African Americans, who were skilled in traditional African healing practices, brought to America. My grandmother was my own birth midwife, and I was born in my grandmother's home in Georgetown.

In *White Fragility: Why It's so Hard for White People to Talk About Racism*, when Robin DiAngelo (2018) speaks of her own possible ancestral experiences, I understand her narrative and cannot help but compare it with my own when viewing it within a racial context. The author says the following:

> I was born into a culture in which I belonged, racially. Indeed, the forces of racism were shaping me even before I took my first breath. If I were born in a hospital, regardless of the decade in which I was born, any hospital would be open to me because my parents were white ... The doctors and nurses attending my birth were in all likelihood white. Although my parents may have been anxious about the birth process, they did not have to worry about how they would be treated by the hospital staff because of their race.
>
> (pp.51–52)

Indeed, the forces of racism were shaping me even before I took my first breath.

Racism was *all* that shaped the life of my first African Diaspora ancestor.

HELEN MORGAN

The Legacy of Slavery

Fanny's commitment to memory and her recognition and respect for her ancestral lineage have led her back through the generations to a dock in Charleston in the 18th century and to her ancestor stepping off the ship that had torn him from his African home. As a white British woman, I too must remember. I too have an ancestral lineage that connects me to that moment and thus interweaves my inheritance with hers. Our ancestral legacies are intimately intertwined, and, if we are to have ordinary conversations about what divides us and where we are the same, this needs honoring.

So let us assume that the ship that had brought that early grandparent to American shores was British. Maybe the ship set sail from London where I live now. Or perhaps it sailed from Bristol where I was born and raised. It was certainly a European vessel. White, European men owned, fitted out, loaded and sailed that ship and thousands like it. White, European men turned the key in the locks and wielded the whips that "danced" the enslaved Africans on the hell that was the journey referred to as the Middle Passage. White, European women wore the fine cotton and sugared their tea, and their men took the snuff and drank the rum all gained from the toil of enslaved Africans. These are my ancestors, and, uncomfortable as it may be, I must acknowledge them.

Investigations that have been undertaken to trace my specific family ancestry do not lead directly to such a ship. However, for a slaving nation such as Britain, this is not the point. The venture—which continued for three centuries—was a collective one. Slave ship owners were not all single merchants. Many small tradesmen had shares in a ship and in the ownership of the slaves who were captured; provided the ship didn't capsize or the slaves die on the way, a considerable profit was to be made.

Such profits benefited not only the individual trader. A 2005 BBC documentary "The Empire Pays Back" emphasized that profits from the trade was only a part of the story. The cities of London, Glasgow, Liverpool and Bristol grew substantially, and European economies were transformed and expanded as a result of the trade and of the slave plantations in the Americas. In his review of the documentary (The Guardian 20.8.2005), Richard Drayton states:

> Profits from slave trading and from sugar, coffee, cotton and tobacco are only a small part of the story. What mattered was how the pull and push from these industries transformed Western Europe's economies. English banking, insurance, shipbuilding, wool and cotton manufacture, copper and iron smelting, and the cities of Bristol, Liverpool and Glasgow, multiplied in response to the direct and indirect stimulus of the slave plantations.

The extent and endurance of the slave trade and colonization and their critical place in the economic development of the West should not be underestimated. It was not merely a matter of a historical aberration. The historian Joseph Miller (2012), in his book *The Problem of Slavery as History*, urges us to view the trans-Atlantic slave trade as part of a whole social process. For, like colonialism, the trans-Atlantic slave trade was not a small-scale industry taking place on the edges of society involving a few traders and sailors. Nor was it just a matter for the plantations on the other side of the Atlantic. Nor can it be safely confined to historical records. This past has a legacy that is evident in the structures within which we live today and in the relative wealth we enjoy. I suggest that this long dark period of our history also has a legacy that reaches into the very soul of our culture, the culture into which we were all born.

While Fanny emphasizes the impact of slavery on the bodies of the enslaved, and hence on the legacy carried by black and brown bodies today, the white body is often missing from the narrative except as split off into the brutal wielder of the whip on the ships or the plantations who can be conveniently isolated from the collective, or into the idealized white female body, which, in stark contrast with the abused black female body, is seen as pure and in need of protection. It has made me wonder whether the white British body escaped entirely the implications of this trauma and, if not, how my ancestors might have been affected.

In his novel, *The Quality of Mercy* set in 18th century Britain, Barry Unsworth (2012) describes how the main character, Kemp, recalls his childhood visiting the Liverpool docks with his father:

> Smells of tar and molasses, and the smell of the slave ships waiting to be loaded with trade goods, a smell unlike any other, a dark odour of blood and excrement: the timbers were impregnated with it, no amount of scrubbing or sluicing had been able to take that smell away ... It had not even been necessary to visit the dock for it, he suddenly remembered; at times it had lain over the whole town. On certain days in summer, with the breezes coming from the west, it had invaded the houses, dark, indefinite, all-pervasive, entering parlours through open windows, contending with the scents of flowers in the gardens.
>
> (pp.95–96)

Unsworth, in the above quote, conjures up scenes of unspeakable horror of what took place aboard those ships, which carry the stink of blood and excrement and which refuse all attempts to sanitize and deny their presence. More, the stench carries across the city into homes "contending with the scents of flowers in the gardens."

One can imagine the ladies and gentlemen of 18th-century Liverpool in their clean and lovely parlors, dressed in imported cotton, drinking sweetened tea, the men perhaps smoking cigars from tobacco leaves cut in the heat of the day by enslaved Africans. In such a scene, the body is sanitized, firmly distanced from the "blood and excrement" of the human cargo of the British ships that plied their trade to bring such refinements to the British gentry.

And yet, in Unsworth's portrayal, the consequences of this trade push their way as only smell can into the lives of the inhabitants of Liverpool rich and poor alike to disturb the peace of those who supported the trade both explicitly and implicitly. The suffering of the African bodies that constituted the ship's cargo in the Middle Passage of a deadly triangle saturated the timbers of the ships waiting in dock, and the stench of such anguish wove its way into the lives of the local citizens and, I suggest, permeates through the ages and haunts the present day.

Transgenerational Transmission of Trauma

Studies of the long-term psychological effects of catastrophic social periods such as the European Holocaust and Stalinism have led to an understanding of how the effects of trauma, if not sufficiently acknowledged and worked through, can be inherited by future generations. Unconscious defenses, established as a means of surviving the trauma, can prevent loss from being taken in, integrated and transformed. Instead, the damage is incorporated as a blockage, which causes stasis and paralysis. In this inorganic, unabsorbed form, it cannot die with those who suffer the trauma but is passed on like a dreadful, undigested legacy to the next generations.

As Stephen Frosh (2013) points out, "One of the things that Holocaust scholarship has demonstrated is how strongly a trauma lived through in one generation continues to have effects in later ones" (p.2). The metaphor of the ghost, of phantoms and haunting is one many writers use to describe this process. Frosh goes on to say:

> To be haunted is more than to be affected by what others tell us directly or do to us openly; it is to be influenced by a kind of inner voice that will not stop speaking and cannot be excised, that keeps cropping up to trouble us and stop us going peaceably on our way, It is to harbor a *presence* that we are aware of, sometimes overwhelmed by, that embodies elements of past experience and future anxiety and hope, and that *will not let us be.*
>
> (pp.2–3, Italics in original)

The Jungian analyst Sam Kimbles, building on his notion of the *cultural complex* he developed with Tom Singer (2004) introduces the hypothesis that intergenerational processes "are manifested as *phantom narratives* that provide structure, representations and continuity for unresolved or unworked-through grief and violence that occurred in a prior historical context that continues into the present" (Kimbles 2014, p.21). He says that the phantom narratives provides an affective field which

> has a narrative structure with (quoting Chomsky, 1958) "deep and buried contents" that operates at the level of the cultural unconscious and is structured by the cultural complexes … It is the unbearable, the too-muchness, the untranslatable, the felt presence of absence that opens the space for phantom narrative.
>
> (Ibid., p.17)

The concept of such an inheritance is developed in Fanny's books "Archetypal Grief: Slavery's Legacy of Intergenerational Child Loss" (2019) and "The Racial Complex: A Jungian Perspective on Culture and Race" (2020).

Gabriele Schwab's (2010) writing as a contemporary German woman of the *"haunting legacy"* of the Holocaust of the 20th century also suggests that, even though the slave trade is further back in time and we are several more generations on, the same mechanisms apply. As Abraham and Torok (1994) put it:

> it is reasonable to maintain that the "phantom effect" progressively fades during its transmission from one generation to the next and that, finally, it disappears. Yet this is not at all the case when shared or complimentary phantoms find a way of being established in social practice.
>
> (p.176)

Racism is the social practice that establishes the phantom effects created by slavery and colonialism within the structures of relating and ensures that the trauma inflicted continues to block integration and healing in the present day.

Legacy for the Perpetrators

Fanny writes powerfully in this chapter of what she carries of the trauma of the African holocaust and how the damage done over centuries to generations of enslaved Africans gathers into a sustained trauma for individuals, families and societies and lies deep within the collective.

My question has to be then, what is it that we who are descendants of the perpetrators have inherited? What is our legacy that we carry within our white psyches? What is the price we pay for this wealth we enjoy? How are we to address the stench of exploitation and abuse that continues to infiltrate the privileged lives of the white British population?

I do not, for one moment, suggest that the legacy is in any way symmetrical. The descendants of the enslaved are burdened with the anguish of lives abused and cut short with all the grief and anger that results; the white population carries the unspoken, unacknowledged shame and guilt of the perpetrators.

Shame and guilt are tricky emotions. On the one hand, guilt is an essential developmental stage for the child to be able to recognize that he or she has done harm to the other, to feel concern and to make reparation. However, when blocked and unconscious, it can so often bring with it anxiety, shame and depression. When there can be no acknowledgement of the act that caused the damage, no confession and therefore no act of reparation, the defenses against the accompanying anxiety become mobilized. Then the guilt is projected onto the other toward whom one feels guilty. Also, because amends cannot be made, the possibility of forgiveness cannot be conceived of. We assume a desire for retaliation from those who have suffered from our acts, and we become fearful that we will be wiped out or overcome by those whom we have injured. When such defenses are active on a collective scale, and when that group holds power over the other, then further attacks may be made on those who are deemed to be causing our troubles.

Healthy guilt may be distinguished from what Stephen Mitchell refers to as "guiltiness." He writes: ".... genuine guilt entails an acceptance of accountability for suffering we have caused others (and ourselves). Without genuine guilt, we cannot risk loving, because the terror of our destructiveness is too great." He goes on to say that "Guilt needs to be distinguished from what we might term 'guiltiness'–perpetual payments in an internal protection racket that can never end" (2000, p.731).

Adrienne Harris (2012) suggests that "guiltiness" might be thought of as guilt in the paranoid-schizoid position:

> The state of alienation and brittle, covered emptiness leaves the person bearing "whiteness" in a double state of knowing and not knowing, depending on a polarized idea of racial identity and at the same time disavowing its falseness, its defensiveness, its empty dangers ... An element in this aspect of white identity, including liberal identities, is an odd, anxious hand-wringing guiltiness.
>
> (p.203)

Mourning and Melancholia

Those who have theorized about the phenomenon of intergenerational trauma suggest that the only way that the sins of the past will cease to haunt the present and future generations is for them to be brought into the open and worked through. Abraham and Torok (1994) call

> for a kind of psychoanalytic "cult of ancestors" ... that allows the dead to rest and the living to gain freedom from their ghostly hauntings. Yet to achieve this freeing from the past requires one first to awaken the dead and to revisit the trauma. This process is what we commonly call mourning. To facilitate a collective mourning, communities and nations develop the need to establish a culture of memory. Recognising the psychic life of our ancestors in our own psychic life means uncovering their unspoken suffering and secret histories, as well as their guilt and shame.
>
> (p.79)

Exploring her relationship to the Holocaust as a German woman, Gabrielle Schwab (2010) suggests that the "transgenerational transmission of collective guilt" is "the identity trouble of children of perpetrators" (p.95). She stresses that

> To facilitate a collective mourning, communities and nations develop the need to establish a culture of memory. Recognizing the psychic life of our ancestors in our own psychic life means uncovering their unspoken suffering and secret histories, as well as their guilt and shame, their crimes.
>
> (p.79)

Once the concept of "race" and the division between "white" and "black" was deployed, the trade in enslaved Africans was underpinned by an assumption of superiority of the "pure," "civilized," "Christian" and "scientific" *white* over the "sinful," "primitive," "pagan" and "irrational" *black,* providing a God-given justification in the European mind.

Looking back, albeit with a different moral emphasis and with our modern concept of human rights, the tragic irony is that the barbarism and savagery belonged to whiteness. If we are to grieve the inhuman acts of our ancestors, we are required to gaze steadfastly into the dark shadows of our white past and articulate the guilt and shame at what we find there. We have to find ways to mourn whiteness itself.

In 2007, Britain celebrated the bicentenary of the Abolition of the Slave Trade Act. While there was a strong and growing protest against the slave trade among the population, largely led by the Quaker movement, it is the politician William Wilberforce who was publicly honored as the central representative of abolition. Identification with this hero—as opposed to those British citizens who feared for their considerable investments and who strongly opposed him—has led to a peculiar collective narrative. The centuries beforehand when Britain plied this horrific trade are not denied—the history is known even if sparsely taught in our schools and only vaguely understood. However, in congratulating ourselves on the abolition of the trade, and shifting the responsibility for the fact that there was anything to be abolished in the first place to a few rogues and deviants on the edges of society, we place ourselves firmly on the side of the angels. We disavow the trade, the traders and our ancestors.

Britain has made no gesture of reparation for our involvement in the trade—not even a statue remembering the enslaved. To date, the charity *Memorial 2007* led by Oku Ekpenyon campaigning for a memorial to slavery for some decades has had no success in getting government support. Writing in The Guardian (2019), Afua Hirsch says:

> this campaign is not requesting a favour for a marginal section of society. The history of how we came to be this nation is a history for us all. If we can't dignify it with a simple memorial, one whose location, design, importance and even planning permission have already been established, then we really have lost the plot.

The word "dignity" in the quote is key here. It was wholly absent from the attitude of the slavers and the plantation owners toward the Africans. Nor did it have any part in the attitude of those who saw the slaves as sinners deserving of their plight. Nor was it present in the 19th-century anthropologists with their hierarchies and their divisions into the "primitive" and the "civilized." Nor of Freud and Jung who lent so heavily on such "armchair Titans." Those who were enslaved may be pitied or feared or disavowed, but as a community, we still refuse them the respect of our grief for what has been done. Their ghosts haunt our collective calling out to be dignified after so many centuries of abusive intimacy and humiliation. If we as a society are to heal, then we must heed and respect their call.

References

Abraham, N. & Torok, M. (1994). *The Shell and the Kernel (Vol. 1)*. Chicago & London: The University of Chicago Press.

Brewster, F. (2019). *Archetypal Grief: Slavery's Legacy of Intergenerational Child Loss*. London & New York: Routledge, Taylor & Francis.

Brewster, F. (2020). *The Racial Complex: A Jungian Perspective on Culture and Race*. Oxon & New York: Routledge.

Drayton, R. (2005). *The Empire Pays Back. Review*. London: The Guardian 20.8.2005.

Duncan, D. (1998). *Calendar: Humanity's Epic Struggle to Determine a True and Accurate Year*. New York: Avon Books.

Frosh, S. (2013). *Hauntings: Psychoanalysis and Ghostly Transmissions*. London: Palgrave Macmillan.

Gottlieb, A. (2004). *The Afterlife Is Where We Come From: The Culture of Infancy in West Africa*. Chicago & London. The University of Chicago Press.

Gyekye, M. (1987). *An Essay on African Philosophical Thought: The Akan Conceptual Scheme*. Cambridge, UK: Cambridge University Press.

Hirsch, A. (2019). Opinion. The Guardian 23.10.2019.

Kimbles, S. (2014). *Phantom Narratives: The Unseen Contributions of Culture to Psyche*. Maryland: Rowman & Littlefield.

Nobles, W.W. (2006). *Seeking the Sakhu: Foundational Writings for an African Psychology*. Chicago: Third World Press.

Schwab, G. (2010). *Haunting Legacies: Violent Histories and Transgenerational Trauma*. New York: Columbia University Press.

Rogers, G.C. (1985). *The History of Georgetown County, South Carolina*. Columbia: University of South Carolina Press.

Singer, T. & Kimbles, S. (Eds.). (2004). *The Cultural Complex. Contemporary Jungian Perspective on Psyche and Society*. Hove & New York: Brunner-Routledge.

Unsworth, B. (2012). *The Quality of Mercy*. London: Windmill Books.

3 The Racial Complex

I imagine the racial complex as a global network, an entangled web of forces laid down over centuries beneath the ground we now stand and move about on, which influences—even controls—our racialized identities and how we think and act in relation to others. Its existence, particularly the more deeply buried aspects that root way back into the history of our ancestors, is often invisible, especially to those of us with whitened eyes.

A consequence of this racist ordering within Western societies is an assumption of whiteness as the default position of the human. Thus, we who are regarded as white may fail to notice how our color affects our sense of identity and the ways we navigate the world and are navigated around by others, taking for granted an entitlement to space, safety and freedom of movement. People of color have largely come to accept that race is a social fact about us all with personal and social repercussions over which we have limited agency, whereas for whites, consideration of the implications of our racial identity is often a new experience. To maintain the illusion of autonomy and control of identity, we don't see the racial complex within which we are all caught, regarding instead any racist act as an individual aberration from which we can dissociate ourselves.

This "white ignorance" as described by Charles Mills (1997) means that the racial complex and its effects may be regarded by white individuals as a feature of life for people of color and for avowed racists. As long as we maintain our liberal "nonracist" view of ourselves, our implication in the complex is denied or ignored and we remain blind and deaf to the part we play in its preservation.

[1]I once visited a training organization as a guest clinician invited to teach as part of a series of clinical seminars for trainees to offer them the experience of a variety of clinical approaches within the psychoanalytic

DOI: 10.4324/9781003025689-4

framework. In each seminar, someone presented their work with a training patient for discussion. The group of trainees came from a variety of professions, and they were experienced and able. While of differing ages and backgrounds, we were all white.

In one seminar, a trainee, Julie, described her work with a 40-year-old woman, Martha, who had come to the United Kingdom from South Africa. She had been referred because of her depression. Julie presented some details about the patient and the work to date including a process report of a particular session. The initial discussion was thoughtful and to the point, and it was apparent that Julie and her colleagues had a good grasp of analytic thinking. After a little while, I realized that the patient's origins had barely been mentioned. I had assumed that the patient was white but didn't know. So I asked and Julie told me the patient was black.

Immediately, the tension in the room was palpable. The group which until then had been working well together with everyone contributing to the thinking froze. When I commented on this, one member of the group said she felt that it was rude to ask about color. The fear seemed to be that even raising the matter was possibly racist.

As someone noted about the area of the country where they lived, "there isn't much ethnic diversity in this part of Britain, so this feels somewhat alien to us." As we discussed this further, people began to express a fear of saying the "wrong" thing or using the "wrong" words betraying a deep anxiety that racist thoughts might be exposed. The lack of racial stamina that DiAngelo describes was much in evidence. It began to be recognized that Julie—indeed all white therapists—had a responsibility to explore their own racism if it was not to infect the work. Gradually, they could think about what it might mean for this black African woman living in such an area and now working with a white therapist. They recognized the need for the therapist to raise the fact of difference so it could be made available for thought. After much discussion, it was suggested that Julie spoke about the matter in a straightforward way within the narrative of the therapy.

Julie reported later that asking what she termed "the white therapist question" had considerable impact on the work. She wrote:

> Although my patient seemed to dismiss its significance, it was noticeable that she then brought material which was a) very culturally specific and b) which led to an increase in affect. Subjectively I felt in the session that there was a sense that the patient was able to entrust this new material with me.

If the patient had been white, any failure to mention it would come from that aspect of white privilege that sees white as the default position—a form of white solipsism. My question made sense in the context that we had been told that the patient came from South Africa, but the assumption of whiteness was understandable given that the large majority of South Africans who have come to Britain and are likely to enter therapy are white. If the patient had been white, the therapist would have said so and we would have moved on without any of the difficulties that the whole group experienced. It is rude, it seems, not so much to raise the question of color per se, but only when the individual is black. It is as if the brown skin is a deformity, a disability, an embarrassment, which is impolite to mention. In therapy, the color muteness that results leaves a gap of silence, which hushes up both an important aspect of the patient's lived experience and of the transferential relationship.

Such discomfort has implications for clinical work where white therapists may struggle to address the matter of racial identity and the impact of racism on the therapeutic relationship. The inclination is to ignore the issue and assume that the transferential dynamics are as color-blind as we claim ourselves to be. It is increasingly recognized that such an approach is at best ineffective and at worst damaging when a white therapist works with a person of color.

The Disavowal of Whiteness

In her important work on the Racial Complex, Fanny Brewster (2020) asks:

> How do we permit the release of the energetic charge of a complex—which may arrive with or without the ego's permission, knowing it increases our fear and anxiety? This is also the clinical work of being with the complex—not always knowing how one will react and even what to do when we have foreknowledge.
>
> (p.14)

The release of the energetic charge of the racial complex is almost always without the white ego's permission because, for white liberals, the anxiety it brings encompasses the potential for both guilt and shame. Eruptions of this complex into consciousness may often be tiny—a slip of the tongue, an unwanted thought, a revealing comment, and the certainty of ourselves as "good," nonracist white people gets rocked for maybe just a moment. Mostly, we rush to close over the gap that has emerged. Mostly, we move on, forget our thought, justify our clumsiness and return to the comfort of "niceness." Yet such moments are key and need to be treasured and explored if we are really to address this complex, the inequality and abuse it causes and our own entrapment in something perverse.

By way of illustration, I turn to a description of my work with Janet, about which I have written elsewhere.

Janet[2]

Janet was a white woman in her late forties who, at the time of the incident described below, had been in analysis with me for several years. She arrived at one session disturbed and shocked. As a social worker in an inner-city area of London, she had been working with a client for some time and had become emotionally close to this young woman of 18 years who she saw as vulnerable and abused. That day, the client, who was also white, had told Janet that she had started a sexual relationship with a black man she had met in a club in the Brixton area of London. Janet's instant, raw reaction to this news had been one of fear and distaste followed by a sense of shame and distress at her own "unthinking" reaction.

Janet considered herself to be a rational liberal person who was used to having black colleagues and friends and thought that she had "worked through" issues of racism. She recognized that her reaction was rooted in a stereotype of a black man and was ashamed of her initial response, which she considered racist. Janet reported the event and the shock of her reaction at the start of the session but hastened to assure me that she had thought it through, and things were OK now. Soon she was on to another subject, and apparently the matter was over and done with.

I was struggling to work out what might be going on here. The recounting of this event had the feel of the confessional, where Janet was telling her secret "sin" to me. It seemed that this was enough, and, with a sigh of relief, we could both move on.

In this, she seemed to be appealing to my understanding as another white woman on two levels. One was a recognition of and familiarity with the stereotypes conjured up by the words "black man" and "Brixton," and the other was a liberalism that had no truck with such silly notions. Both expectations were accurate. The questions in my mind were: What was her immediate response in terms of her internal world? What was she defending against in the shame and the wish to move on? What was being reenacted in the transference?

Despite an uncomfortable feeling in the room, I returned to the subject of the client's boyfriend and the apparent avoidance of any further thinking about the matter. Struggling with feelings of shame and embarrassment, Janet began to articulate her associations more explicitly.

Until the rapid rise in house prices in the inner city, Brixton had been an area of London where the majority population was of African-Caribbean descent, and for Janet it represented London's "Heart of Darkness," a vibrant but fearful place, which both repelled and fascinated her. Locating this black man in Brixton increased a sense of both excitement and dread. Janet imagined this man to be sexually active and attractive, and she was able to acknowledge both her fear of him as threat and her envy of the client having this exciting sexual object. She had already imagined the man making the young woman pregnant and then abandoning her. The fear of the aggressive, contaminating and feckless phallic male was evident.

Along with some complex processes that were specific to the internal world of my patient, a few main themes emerged relevant to the subject of whiteness. One was the projection of an animal male sexuality onto the man and an innocent pure femininity onto the client who had to be protected. But there was also her sense of "badness" and shame at having these aggressive and penetrating thoughts. Despite her commitment to antiracist practice, she was still capable of such "bad" thoughts, which had intruded into her mind like an aggressive attack. In themselves they were shadow aspects that penetrated, left her with a shitty baby and then abandoned her. The client, perceived as the victim of the black man, was "innocent" and "pure" of such nasty notions.

Despite the urge to dismiss them from her mind and forget that they ever arose, these responses were sufficiently troubling for her to bring them to her therapy and speak them out loud. She understood that the initial reaction expressed an internal state that she wished, at least in part, to explore with me. However, the reporting of her subsequent thinking and the moving on to other topics suggested an invitation to conspire both with her initial disgust and with her subsequent shame. Her "confession" followed by the response "it's all right now" seemed to be an appeal for me to ally myself with the aggressive intruding thought, the innocent female victim and the rescuer who protected my patient from this attack by denial and silence.

This invitation to collude was tempting. I recognized both the initial response and the shame it provoked, making it all too easy and far more comfortable to let the session move on to some other subject. While these responses may have been used unconsciously by my patient to support her avoidance, they were not only counter-transference responses for they included more general processes familiar to me as a white individual living in a white racist society. What was going on here?

Disavowal

There is now a substantial body of research establishing that children learn about racial structures very early—as young as three years old. The process seems to be top-down whereby the child learns that there are discriminating social dynamics that disadvantage those from some groups and privilege others. Only then do they learn what those groups are and who belongs to them.

When white children raise their queries about racial inequalities, many white adults become embarrassed, hush the child, ignore or distract them and resort to the shortcut of color-blindness by insisting that everyone is the same and equal. Such an assertion is not only untrue and denies what the child observes and experiences but also by focusing on the universality of humans, the message is conveyed that it is the *recognition* of difference that is the cause of racism rather than the fact that the child has been born into a social system that discriminates against certain groups, which they need help to acknowledge, understand and respond to.

Thus, two conflicting realities must exist side by side. Awareness of racist structures, white advantage and one's own racist thoughts lie on one side of the divide and the investment in being "good" (i.e., not a racist) on the other. To manage this tension, the defense of disavowal is brought into play.

Disavowal develops within the ego when it is faced with two conflicting realities causing a vertical split. Unlike repression, the individual remains conscious of both sides of the split but will disavow either to meet internal desires and needs or to minimize anxiety. In relation to race, I have come to imagine this particular psychic structure as two vertical layers between which there is a gap, a silent, empty place devoid of symbols in which it is impossible to play or grieve.

When Janet related the incident with her client and her initial racist responses, her "misbehavior," she did so with no sense of justification or excuse. These thoughts were regarded as "racist" and "wrong," and as such, I was expected to join with her in condemning them. However, the invitation to conspire with her, to not take them seriously enough to talk about to bury them without mourning, repeated a process that I suspect began when she was young.

The challenge to the therapist when faced with vertical forms of splitting is always considerable for the work of integration requires movement both vertically to unconscious material and horizontally across the disavowed aspects. However, it is especially difficult when there is a split in the therapist that matches that of the patient. There is no reason to believe that I as a white woman raised in a white racist society with liberal parents experienced anything fundamentally different in my early years regarding race than Janet had. Both the unconscious acceptance of racism and its condemnation created the same vertical split within me. I had no trouble understanding both Janet's original thoughts and their rejection, as well as the seeking of the confessional and the absolving of the sin via a conspiracy of silence.

But the liberal position is complex and entangled. If the mechanism of denial was complete, Janet may have entirely ignored or "forgotten" her initial reactions and they would not have been mentioned. Part of the motivation for doing so may be seen as a way of seeking absolution through my identificatory silence, but she was also genuinely troubled by her initial reaction and was open to working with me to explore it further. While the disavowal mechanism has early roots, it exists alongside an honest concern for the other, as well as a commitment to fairness, equality and human rights—all central features of liberalism. The child may learn and incorporate the dead response she meets, but it is a loss and the lack will be felt. "Guiltiness" cohabits alongside healthy, appropriate guilt with its desire to make reparation; they both need recognition.

The mechanism of disavowal is often so efficient and swift that thoughts betraying internal racist structures may hardly be noticed and rapidly forgotten. Attention is needed to catch them as they arise so they can become available for study. Janet's responses had been sufficiently strong and troubling to stay with her and to tell me, but effort on both our parts was needed to return to them. The deadness, the anxious silence of the gap in the structure of disavowal refuses symbolization making analytic work impossible from that place. But we *could* elaborate the defenses on either side of the gap where free association and imagination remained viable, so that we were gradually able to talk about the silent, dead space from a place of life.

FANNY BREWSTER

Mirroring the Transference

The initial title for my section of this chapter was "Being with my Other." Then I wondered about perpetuating the idea of an "Other." How much does it hurt *all* others and does it keep us separate from one another not only in the language of aloneness but equally in our desire to gain authentic intimacy in relationships? Yet I do think I understand the things that can keep us apart as being not only survival-oriented tribal—this is almost innate to our nature. I also consider the cultural aspects of relationships in terms of how the culture of psychoanalysis itself was developed for a "two-some." This is not necessarily injurious; it is only how it began. How do we wish for the classical dyad to continue? If the transference—the projections onto the other within the clinical setting happen in a natural way, does it have its own propensity to eventually create separation? How does the racial complex, this one certainly being a collective "hinge" one in the American unconscious, become activated within the transferential analytical relationship? It would appear that a racial complex would be a significant influential factor in this relationship of different or even mutual ethnicities of the analytical dyad (Brewster 2020).

In this chapter on the Transference, I'm considering it within a cultural as well as a clinical context. There has always been an assumption of *whiteness* as we speak about the transferential relationship in the temenos. The sacredness of the clinical office in Jungian practice was established with the culture of whiteness as a preconceived fact. It was just assumed. The accoutrements were white—the analysis, the doctors and the patients. In the imagination, whiteness dominated and still can.

The healing arts from an Africanist tradition was considered by most 19th-century colonizers to be "witchcraft," "taboo." At the time of the emergence of "modern psychology," the medical practices of the "Other" indigenous people were set in an oppositional frame that addressed them as "hoodoo" and without value. The medicine of the "Other," rooted in philosophical and spiritual beliefs, was declared worthless.

The Transference as an aspect of Jungian psychological work helps focus the relationship between the analyst and the analysand. It provides a structure and a way in which the analyst can understand the nature of what is occurring between herself and the analysand, the other. What are the influences in this work when each is of a different ethnicity? In the case of a black individual with a white analyst, it would be impossible to not think about ethnic differences. The long historical events of a Middle Passage and racism exhibited through the generations causing intergenerational trauma would exist within the phenomenological field. Throughout the training to become an analyst, the importance of the Transference is stressed. *Projection*, a necessary element of the Transference, is a part of ego conscious awareness that develops between analyst and analysand.

The ability to speak together regarding what the analyst might be receiving in terms of projections from the analysand deepens the relationship. Without these projections and the intimacy that develops with their exploration, the psychological work can become stymied and almost artificial. At some point in the work, both individuals realize that they are holding some ideas, concerns and/or fantasies about the person they meet weekly, perhaps for years. The time spent on discussing not only the analysand's projections in the temenos but also outside in other relationships, past and present, supports building ego strength.

With this strength, the analysand can take increased responsibility for the life and the ways in which to live it more creatively, safely, bountifully. Realization comes that an Other is not at fault, to blame for what happens "to" the analysand. In the language of the work, the analysand learns how to "pull back" the projections, examine them as aspects of her own psychological needs and integrates how to satisfy the self without demanding that another hold responsibility.

The moment of self-realization within the clinical work as projections is realized to belong to oneself, not what someone is doing "to" you is extraordinary, perhaps epiphany-like because now there is so much more freedom in choosing how one wants to truly live. More conscious power now resides within the individual.

How does the Transference and its accompanying projections coexist when culture is a factor? This is a question that has not been necessary to ask, to consider, within American Jungian Psychology for most of the years that it has been practiced—approximately 100 years. In the course of this century, much has changed in the lives of Africanist people. Yet much remains the same. In general, within the broad collective, racial relationships are never fully understood on a deep psychological level. The lack of tolerance, the avoidance of painful interracial discussions and the ongoing racist intergenerational projections onto an "Other" have assisted in the continuation of racism in a variety of ways through centuries. In our most recent times, we have witnessed murders of Africanist individuals by law enforcement on a yearly basis. The death of George Floyd has been the most profoundly disturbing murder of an Africanist individual in the past year. In thinking about a *racial complex*, we can investigate how projections onto an ethnically different Other can be enacted through negative behaviors.

This identifies events that have been displayed through years of racist actions within American society. The constellation of a racial complex within the individual as well as the collective keeps our cultural awareness of the need for kinship *within* our group more alive and desirable. How might this be enacted in the temenos between a black analysand and a white analyst?

We must reconsider how we have thought about and practiced Jungian psychology in terms of the African Diaspora. This is particularly true in non-European settings, such as America, where cultural attributes have been ignored.

However, I will add that Jung saw cultural differences but did not necessarily wish to include these Africanist cultural attributes as valuable to the practice of American Jungian psychology. This has been an unfortunate circumstance since America represents a country that is ethnically diverse. In rethinking 19th-century psychology theories, it is essential to analyze their applicability in classically practiced forms to those of the African Diaspora. This is specifically because the psychological theories formulated inherently included racist ideas regarding Africanist people. Equally important is that the beginning medical practices of American doctors, including psychiatry, used the bodies of Africanist people for experimentation to the detriment of this cultural group.

The distrust that exists within the Africanist cultural group has taken time to lessen. It is not completely resolved as shown by the most recent reluctance on the part of many black community members to take the vaccine developed to combat the CORONA-19 virus. There is a kind of anxiety that is specific to African Diaspora individuals moving toward and engaging in mental health services and medical care in general that remain dominated by white society.

The absence of Africanist people seeking mental services within a basically white psychiatric establishment has its own tragic history. In *The Protest Psychosis: How Schizophrenia Became a Black Disease* (2009), the author, Jonathan Metzl, highlights aspects of this history.

Returning to the work of the psychological clinical setting and the concept of Transference and projections, I propose that there is no way to ignore culture differences between analyst and analysand. There is also no means to blindly look beyond the intergenerational trauma of African Diaspora individuals. What then does this mean for black individuals who seek out psychological treatment from a white Jungian analyst?

The historical pattern has been to avoid engagement—on the part of potential analysands and also perhaps analysts. I will say that the treatment expense associated with Jungian psychology can be almost prohibitive. Another factor is the generally known racial bias that can be read in the language of Jung's *Collected Works* in his discussion of Africanist people. His ambivalence in the 1930s toward Nazism has been noted, discussed, as well as dismissed, to a varying degree within the Jungian analytical community.

The beginning of any analysis has anxiety as a part of its nature. Individuals make their initial call reaching out to the analyst. It is only natural to feel some anxiety in asking for help of a stranger. This is the beginning of the Transference, or it may have already happened as technology allows individuals to "see" into the life of the analyst before actually emailing or calling for an initial appointment. It may have happened in the dreaming life before or after the initial call. Is the unconscious showing potentiality of the Transference? This anxiety and oftentimes accompanying relief at finding someone begins the analytical relationship. What are the projections brought into this analytical moment and how does ethnicity fit into it when the analyst is white and the analysand is black or of a different ethnicity?

This is the current situation that American Jungian psychology has for the most part never had to encounter. When Jung came to America on his one trip that involved a one-month dream research encounter with black men at St. Elizabeth's Hospital in Washington, D.C., there was never any consideration of Jung providing clinical work with these men or any other members of the African Diaspora. His opinion was that one of the men's dream was important to be used in establishing his theory of the universality of the collective unconscious (Brewster 2017). However, Jung in the totality of this theory purported that Africanist people were "lowest" on the scale of human consciousness.

The underlying proposition was that they would be unable to receive the "benefits" of psychoanalysis due to their lowered level of consciousness. This reminds me of a co-authored book by Stein and Grazine entitled *Confronting Cultural Trauma: Jungian Approaches to Understanding and Healing* (2014). Though this book covers the cultural trauma of groups of people around the world and there is an essay on South Africa and apartheid, there is no mention of the African Holocaust, the cultural trauma of African Americans, South Americans or Caribbean people. It is as if Africanist people, the Diaspora, do not exist in relationship to American Jungian psychology. This could be almost true except for Jung's early writings about the African individuals who were his guides and confidents on his trips to Africa, dreaming about his African American barber and his dream study of black men at St. Elizabeth's Hospital in 1913.

It is the emergence of new thinking that is necessary to reflect on the possible nature of a Transference between a variety of ethnic individuals doing psychological work within the Jungian clinical setting. This *is* the current state of affairs. The 19th-century world that created early European and American psychoanalysis is gone; evidence of colonial racism has shifted into the shadow in the form of unconscious racism, institutional and structural racism, a recognition of the "privilege" and "fragility" of cultural whiteness. How does unconscious racism show itself within the temenos and with white psychoanalysts working psychologically with individuals of color? This is a question being asked more often now than ever before as individuals of color, BIPOCS, can begin to seek out mental health services, including psychoanalysis, understanding the need for healing of trauma and emotional suffering.

How does the established structures of psychanalytical institutes, training 21st-century clinicians, created on biased Eurocentric psychological theories support individuals of color seeking to train and become analysands within these institutes?

These are all questions of significance that affect not only individuals seeking psychological work but also the very integrity of the training of analytical candidates and those who have built and maintain the institutes. In returning to the Transference and viewing its importance in clinical work, it is of equal importance to see how all parts of the psychological work interconnect with one another. It is not only about the relationship of an "Other" but also the history, culture and contemporary building blocks that make up the specialization of psychoanalysis within American psychology. These all become influential factors in the energetic field of the Transference. The assumptions of whiteness that shaped American psychoanalysis cannot be embraced in its customary manner. Too much time has passed and too much has taken place in our American society to keep us from creating new pathways of understanding our psychological selves. This includes politics and the cultural impact of necessary changes in the collective in terms of understanding racism and social justice.

In the moment of meeting a person of color within the temenos, I am aware that our cultural experiences will be a natural part of shaping the clinical work that will develop. I do believe that this is an understood guiding principle of psychoanalytical work that has existed between a white analyst and an analysand for a century. Those who might argue that culture and politics have no place in the temenos setting do not have the sensibilities of being a person of color in a racialized collective. Identity is as important to the person of color outside the temenos as it is within the clinical setting.

The identity of being white has the privilege of not needing to state belonging—it is understood, it is assumed. This is the same within the temenos. The work of psychology and psychoanalysis is to create a space for the acceptance of an unapologetic black identity. The multitude of false narratives created about black people contains almost uncountable racial projections.

Many of these projections might be considered under the heading of a racial complex. This complex and its identification give both analysand and analyst a place to begin speaking of the Transference and projections within the psychological work. When whiteness is presupposed, what possible disruption to the work of psyche occurs in the Transference between a white and a historically ethnically different Other?

Recognizing that racism exists remains an emotionally painful circumstance for many Africanist people and has been so for centuries. The racism that is a part of a racial complex has an emotional body that belongs to the individual for whom the complex becomes activated. The existence of complexes and their accompanying emotions are identified by the analyst and eventually by the analysand as psychological work begins and continues. A meaningful aspect of this work between individuals of differing ethnic identities could be discussions regarding the racial complex and its significance within the Transference. This is an element of the emotional *discomfort* most often spoken of by white analysts who address the unknown territory of venturing into a discussion of raciality with individuals of color within the clinical setting.

A major hesitancy is not having the language to know what to say, how to begin to enter a clinical conversation of race, racism and racial relations. The mirrored transferential movement for the individual of color is feeling this discomfort and not knowing how and/or not wishing to "save" the analytical moment from some sort of failure. What happens to the Transference at this moment? The clinical work of integration of culture into the psychological moment is just beginning with white psychoanalysis and people of color. The voice of members of the African Diaspora when expressed says that the whiteness of psychoanalysis does not see them, cannot see them and does not include their cultural identity of blackness.

This is true for different reasons and cannot be ignored if psychoanalysis wishes to be inclusionary. Its history has mostly been one of class and racial exclusion and can oftentimes still appear to wear this mantle to those in training to become psychoanalysts, no matter their ethnicity. The answers to such complexity are still not apparent to those engaged in working within the field of psychology. Since the Transference remains a key component of clinical work, it appears to demand our attention as a part of working through issues of *othering* unconscious racism in the form of projections, racial complexes and emotional anxieties caused by the presence of an ethnically different other.

Notes

1 This example is from Morgan, H. (2021). *The Work of Whiteness: A Psychoanalytic Perspective*. Oxford: Routledge (pp.19–20).
2 This example first appeared in Morgan, H. (2014). Between Fear and Blindness: The White Therapist and the Black Patient. In *Thinking Space: Promoting Thinking About Race, Culture, and Diversity in Psychotherapy and Beyond*. Ed: Lowe, F. London: Karnac.

References

Brewster, F. (2020). *The Racial Complex: A Jungian Perspective on Culture and Race*. London: Routledge.
Grazine, G. & Stein, M. (Eds.). (2014). *Confronting Cultural Trauma: Jungian Approaches to Understanding and Healing*. New Orleans: Spring Journal.
Metzl, J. (2009). *The Protest Psychosis: How Schizophrenia Became a Black Disease*. Boston: Beacon Press.
Mills, C. (1997). *The Racial Contract*. Ithaca, NY: Cornell University Press.
Morgan, H. (2014). Between fear and blindness. *Thinking Space: Promoting Thinking About Race, Culture, and Diversity in Psychotherapy and Beyond*. Ed: Lowe, F. London. Karnac.

4 The Creation of the *Other*
Modern Psychology and Its Influences

The Dreamlife

In this chapter, my interest in the study of dreams guides my discussion. The practice and theoretical system of psychoanalysis, with dreamwork as a key component, has ingrained in it, a European creation of, and racial bias against, an Africanist "Other." The beginning of all psychological work, for example, traditional African medicine, Freudian and Jungian dreamwork, or Carl Rogers's person-oriented therapy occurred within a particular cultural group. However, dreaming is universal, and it is this *cultural universality*, and not the sociological racial biases of society, that must gain further acceptance in the field of psychology. When Jung developed his theory of the Collective Unconscious, of which dreamwork can be an essential aspect, he spoke of the universality of the theory. However, over time we can note flaws in his model, as Africanist people were placed at the lower end of his *consciousness hierarchy* including Jung's study of the dreamlife.

Universality as initially theorized by Jung was actually a contradiction since it could not, according to Jung, actually embrace Africanist people except in a rigidly held "bottom" position from which they could never move into individuating, deepening consciousness in the life span. All of Jung's ideas that developed from his theory of a Collective Unconscious eliminated Africans and the African Diaspora except within the category of a "deprived" Other, when compared with endowed white society members. In this way, the establishment of 19th-century modern psychology meant creating an opposite Other within psychological theories. This included the study of dreams and the taking of some attributes of Africanist cultural ideas—cultural appropriation, but never a theoretical inclusion of Africanist peoples' dreamlife as having a cultural or "collective" value. Modern psychology as practiced in America emerged from 19th-century Europe primarily through the research and studies of Sigmund Freud. C.G. Jung as an early follower and colleague of Freud was initially thought to be his heir apparent. Their relationship began with enthusiasm and an intense comradery regarding interest in the unconscious. Jung eventually broke with Freud developing psychological theories that explored human consciousness and the unconscious through nondrive and nonbiological theories. Freud and Jung's bitter separation led to Jung developing his own practice of what he called Analytical Psychology that included a major emphasis on the study of the unconscious. From this focus, Jung became deeply interested in the dreams of the unconscious and developed a theory of the Collective Unconscious that was also inclusive of mythology. Over time, Jung's idea that archetypal patterns existed within the unconscious, shaping and holding the human ego consciousness, grew in societal acceptance.

Jung began his early work with mentally ill patients in Burgholzli Hospital in Zurich. He eventually developed a private practice in which archetypal psychology, with its focus on dream analysis, and issues of Transference and counter transference came to dominate his work.

Jung spent many years analyzing the dreams of Europeans. Over time, Jung's Analytical Psychology with its focus on the study of dreams, and his belief regarding mythological influences on archetypes, were recognized by other European men who were developing their own theories in the newly emerging field of psychology.

The Dream in Primitive Cultures (Lincoln 1935) was one of the most informative Eurocentric texts on the attitude toward and status of the dreamlife of Africans following the last wave of colonialism at the turn of the 19th century.

Lincoln's study of African dreams is based primarily on the work of Sigmund Freud, although Carl Jung's early exploration into the importance of manifest versus latent content of native people's dreamlife was reviewed. The most credence and respect were given to Freud's thinking as expressed in *The Interpretation of Dreams*. Lincoln in his critique of Jung states, "Jung ... denies that fantasy is just the disguised expression of repressed unconscious wishes, and he has undergone a kind of animistic regression towards a *primitive* attitude with regard to fantasy" (p.89).

The word *primitive* is used in the field of psychology to mean that which is undeveloped. Generally, it carries a negative connotation. Often it is placed opposite a strong, developed ego in the hierarchy of psychological development. As a rule, "primitive" is applicable to any ancient or original person or circumstance. Even today, indigenous people all over the world are often called primitive. In fact, European writers in the first half of this century may still refer to Africanist peoples, Native Americans and other indigenous groups as primitives. Although the term may have initially denoted ancient or original, within 19th-century colonialism, it clearly connoted uncivilized, unintelligent and even ignorant—in other words, the presumed opposite of European civilization, intelligence and knowledge. Using such prejudicial descriptors, Europeans justified their invasion and confiscation of foreign lands, including much of Black Africa, and ultimately their self-serving classicist hierarchy, which placed all those designated as primitive, including Africans, on the bottom rung of the ladder of human civilization.

As a consequence of this cultural bigotry, Christian missionaries attempted to dissuade African people from their own ancient cosmological beliefs in a life continuum with spiritual beings and ancestors. Europeans and American Christian missionaries thus tried to turn Africans away from their own ancestor reverence, healing traditions (which almost always included divination) and spiritual practices that honored goddesses and gods. Indigenous African spiritual customs and healing practices were very much intertwined. Sickness, healing and spirituality were integral aspects of a single cosmology. The traditional healer's divination could ascertain the divine, ancestral cause of sickness and prescribe a healing solution. Into this ancient, well-integrated cultural ethos, Europeans brought the priest, the confessional and the concept that sickness was caused by germs, or by offending God the Father. Absolution and healing were now to be in the hands of the priest or the European doctor.

Modern depth psychology grew directly out of prejudices that Freud, Jung and other early depth psychologists claimed through the writings of European "explorers" of Africa. Though Freud, like others of his day, spent no actual time with indigenous people and conducted no analysis or treatment with them, he decided that he was able to write about their psychology in *Totem and Taboo* (1913). Freud and others were assisted by anthropologists such as Lucien Levy-Bruhl, Claude Levi-Strauss and Mircea Eliade, men who built their professional careers writing about indigenous peoples. Because of the writings of these men and others like them, V. Mudimbe (1994) states in *The Idea of Africa* that it was determined how Africa would be imaged and projected onto world consciousness—namely, that Africa and Africans were to be seen as *prelogical*, as uncivilized and of low intellect. This racist construction exists in one form or another in much of the early social science literature from missionary studies of Africans, such as *Bantu Philosophy* (Temples, 1945), through and including American literature of the 20th century, *The Bell Curve: Intelligence and Class Structure in American Life* (Herrnstein & Murray 1994).

Though Jung traveled to Africa and described his visit there as an awakening of his own consciousness, he committed a bare fraction of his writings to Africanist people.

His writings about Africanist peoples, including African Americans with whom he completed minimal dream research—one month, appear for the most part racist and prejudicial. (Brewster 2013) For example, in his autobiography *Memories, Dreams, Reflections* (1973), Jung describes his 1925 journey to Africa. In one comment, he observes the wife of Elgonyis, his African guide, and Jung describes his own thinking regarding Africans. He writes: "What goes on in the interior of these 'simple' souls is not conscious, is therefore unknown, and we can only deduce it from comparative evidence of advanced European differentiation" (p.263).

This notion of "simple souls," Africans who were incapable of *consciousness*, continues within psychological circles as applied to differences between African Americans and whites. As recently as the late 20th century, two Harvard psychology professors (Herrnstein & Murray 1994) claimed to have documented that African Americans are less intelligent than whites and that there is no remedy for this situation. It would appear that not only in the realm of dream studies but also in the field of psychology as a whole that intellectual bigotry has not changed much in the 70 years since Jung's trip to Africa and the more than 100 years since Freud's *The Interpretation of Dreams* (2009).

Given these circumstances, it is especially ironic that some of what Jung developed into Analytical Psychology reflects the traditional beliefs and customs of Africanist people. In spite of Jung's own disparaging attitudinal writings about African people, it seems apparent that in developing certain aspects of his Analytical Psychology, he actually borrowed from indigenous peoples' customs and ways—for example, in his idea of participation mystique (Levy-Bruhl's law of participation) and of dreams as indicators in psychic healing and life direction. Jung acknowledged Africans as the "primitive" contributors of major beliefs incorporated into his theories of Analytical Psychology.

Jung (1977), speaking of his dreams and the guidance he gets from them, says, "I am as primitive as any nigger, because I do not know!" (p.286). In this way, Jung indicated that he, like Africans, are guided by dreams, and his ethnicity does not assure him of having prior knowledge as regards dreaming. Still, even with such tacit and stated demeaning indebtedness to African people, Jung warned white Americans of the dangers of being influenced by African Americans, noting that the language and music (Jazz) of African Americans had already negatively affected the behavior of whites. He even assured white Americans that due to their own large demographic numbers, as compared with blacks, they need not yet worry about being overcome by the latter.

Levy-Bruhl, in a manner similar to Freud, wrote partially to counter the influence of rationalism in European society. The former's emphasis on finding a community of individuals who Europeans could emulate for their "emotionalism" was readily welcomed in the early years of the 20th century. This cultural community became Africans. One of the most important points in Levy-Bruhl's writing is his idea of the inability of Africans to reason. This idea did not originate with Levy-Bruhl. However, it is from his theories that others, including Jung, have developed psychological theories. The idea that Africanist people are the primary carriers of emotions and instinct has been brought forward as a part of racial *social mythology* surrounding Africanist people. Levy-Bruhl sought a way to promote his own theories regarding Africans. He found a formula describing the thinking and feelings of Africans that was more acceptable by European society and unfortunately more psychologically and culturally destructive for Africanist people.

Levy-Bruhl's perspective on African myths primarily focused on the myth as agent for "solidarity" and thinking function within African communities.

Partly because of this theoretical idea, Africanist individuals are considered unable to reason. I find most disturbing the power and the influence this idea has had for a century. I have heard it argued that Levy-Bruhl was no different from others of his time in formulating theories regarding Africanist people. However, I believe that his theory has been one of the most damaging in terms of the basis for formulation of psychological theories, and their applicability to Africanist people.

African American Mythology, Spirituality and the Dreamlife

I believe that there are several threads of spiritual practice operative among African Americans. In the last –25 years, many individuals are actively seeking a closer identity and involvement with African-oriented spiritual practices. These include practioners of Santeria, Voudou and Yoruba. Others continue in the protestant religion of their family and African American ancestors. Women such as Harriet Tubman and Sojourner Truth were converted to Protestant religions but appeared to speak with the spirit of the Orisha. There is a questioning unrest regarding traditional Protestantism among African Americans, which

Modern Psychology and Its Influences 69

is reflected in loss of membership by the traditional church to those seeking a more "charismatic" or neo-Pentecostal interpretation of their faith. In *The Black Church in the African American Experience*, authors Lincoln and Mamiya (1990) define this loss of membership in their chapter "Challenges to the Black Church." Factors influencing this decline include those African American men who choose to become Muslim and follow the Islamic religion. A lack of church growth is attributed to the absence of young adults, primarily male, considered without church affiliation, the "unchurched."

A third factor is the current political and economic climate in America, which began providing support typically given within the African American church. As professional African Americans move into the middle class, the church is viewed less as an economic, social and political necessity than in former times. I have not seen studies that draw correlations between levels of discontent and a lack of connection based on spiritual lineage but I am curious with regard to this possibility.

Henry Gates (1988) in *The Signifying Monkey* explores Esu/Legba, a mythological god from the Yoruba tradition. Gates defines mythology, using Esu as a definitive model. He states that Africans did not arrive in America as "tabula rasa" but with the cultures of their heritage. Esu's survival in the New World is evidence of this transport of culture. Gates describes Esu as messenger of the gods. Like Hermes, the Greek messenger god, Esu travels between the gods and humans, living, as Gates says, with "one leg in each realm." In this role, he survives in countless mythologies serving not only as messenger but also as trickster god, creating chaos and confusion. In his more spiritual function, Esu is able to "read the signs" of Ifa divination as taught to him by Ifa. Esu serves as divine interpreter of the Ifa oracle. Esu interprets to humans for the gods. The reading of "signs" includes dreams and the study of dreaming. If it is true that we bring forward our ancestral/archetypal patterns, how might they show themselves in today's religious practice in terms of dreaming? What of the integrative spiritual practices of African Americans and how does the dreaming life influence these practices? How might the practices evolve, given a more positive point of view, without racialized 19th-century psychological theories? Where is Esu's place in contemporary spiritual practice as an aspect of Africanist unconsciousness and dreaming?

Esu, who is sometimes known as Legba, acquired a monkey as companion when brought to the Americas during slavery. This monkey appears to have become the possessor of the "tricks" for which Esu was known for in Africa. Author Gates notes that Esu is known for his duality.

He is distinguished among the Yoruba gods for confusion and returning during the most passionate, embittered exchange to offer a rational, calming solution to a problem he himself has created. Esu is both male and female. He is an unknown factor and always creates uncertainty wherever he goes. One of his greatest powers is his ability is to connect with and interpret life's events. Dream interpretation becomes an area of possession under Esu's guidance.

According to Yoruba tradition, just before birth we are given knowledge, through our "ori" (head) of who we are to become. We choose the life we are to live. At birth, we forget these choices and Ifa divination serves to help remember one's destiny. Esu is the mythological god who serves as mediator in this spiritual task. As one seeks understanding and interpretation of myth, author Gates suggests that it is through Esu that one can expect to find answers as well as divine knowledge. Dreaming is the most important aspect of gaining knowledge through the unconscious as well as family and the ancestors (Bynum 2017).

> In Africa, the importance of dreams, and family dreams, also has a long cultural, clinical, and psychospiritual history. It is a given in many religious societies that family members, both living and deceased, and also the gods themselves, can and do communicate with the dreamer in the dream. This belief greatly expands the personal matrix of experience, causality, and time flows since this extended family unconscious system enfolds not only the generation to be born and the currently living but also up to five generations of the departed.
>
> (*The Dreamlife of Families*, p.29)

In understanding that there is a spiritual path and a god who delivers us the dream message, it is significant to include African mythology in the realm of other gods who may "visit" during our sleeping hours.

African Americans have a spiritual tradition that is strong even though traditional African slave spiritual practices were forbidden by slavers. These culturally different practices were held to be demonic or heathen. In accommodating themselves to their new environment, these first Africans incorporated the slaveholder's Christian religious beliefs into their own. Today, in different parts of North America, there are communities of Ifa, a Yoruba religion of Nigeria. In Ifa, divination continues as a spiritual practice as it has for centuries. The babalawo, assisted by Esu and others of the Orisha, provides spiritual direction.

This African religion has maintained the character of African origin without much influence from European religion. Other religions of

Africanist people such as Baptist, Pentecostal and AME more clearly show this influence. The importance of the inclusion of Africanist dreaming must be highlighted due to its significant racially *biased inclusion* in 19th-century modern psychology. Dreaming and studies of the dreamlife were and continue to be essential parts of African traditional healing practices and, therefore, its psychology. It is noted that most often when African dreams were included in any discussion within early modern psychology, it was with profound racial negativity as to the customs and cultural aspects of Africanist dreaming. In our contemporary practice of psychology, we must be aware of the racialized foundations of modern psychology. We continue to include dreaming and dreamwork as important psychological processes of the unconscious, as the most important elements of our clinical work. We must acknowledge how the field of psychology developed and its initial creation of institutional racism into its societal structure. This has included within Jungian dreamwork psychology negative theories of Africanist people and the Shadow of racism. This is what we engage with now—the history, and the intention to see and provide new narratives of racial equity to 21st-century conversations of psychoanalysis.

HELEN MORGAN[1]

Born at the end of the 19th century when Europe dominated much of the world and the trade in African slaves had not long been abolished, psychoanalysis, with its key concepts of the unconscious, the id, infantile sexuality, and so on, placed the "heart of darkness" deep within the psyche of all humans, including the colonizer. In so doing, Freud potentially challenged the accepted division between the "civilized" white European and the so-called "primitive" indigenous populations. On the one hand, by demonstrating the tenuousness of the power of the rational ego, it subverts the European Enlightenment view with its emphasis on science, rationality and control. Such a view legitimized binary, oppositional thinking, which became incorporated into the structuring of the social and political system, heralding an alienation from the natural world.

On the other hand, as Hillman (1986) points out:

> The convention informing geographical discoveries and the expansion of white consciousness over Africa continues to inform psychic geography. The topological language used by Freud for "the unconscious" as a place below, different, timeless, primordial, libidinal and

separated from consciousness, recapitulates what white reporters centuries earlier said about West Africa. Part of psychology's myth is that the unconscious was "discovered" as its contents are "explored." Even the notion of the underworld as black rather that grayish, misty or invisible bespeaks white supremacy.

Moreover, the "discovery" of an unconscious separate from consciousness, as a black continent separated from white penetration into it, maintains the very unconsciousness within white which the idea was invented to wound.

(pp.45–46)

The "Primitive"

Both Freud and Jung relied heavily on the early anthropologists, the so-called "armchair titans" of the 19th century, such as Taylor, Haeckel and Lamarck. Taking their theories of human hierarchies, the inheritability of acquired characteristics, the assumption of European "civilization" and the "barbarism" of the colonized, as well as Haeckel's theory that "ontology recapitulates phylogeny," both men regarded the black "primitive" as representing

- the early stages of the development of the European,
- the "uncivilized," unrepressed id contents of the Western psyche, and
- the mind of the European infant.

There are men still living who, as we believe, stand very near to primitive man, far nearer than we do, and whom we therefore regard as his direct heirs and representatives. Such is our view of those whom we describe as savages or half-savages, and their mental life must have a particular interest for us if we are right in seeing in it a well-preserved picture of an early stage of our own development (Freud 1913, p.53).

The adoption of these ideas by Freud and Jung was not inevitable. In the early part of the 20th century, there were those who criticized this way of thinking and offered alternative constructions. For example, as Andrew Samuels points out, Franz Boas, considered the father of American anthropology, was well known at the start of the century. Referencing Sonu Shamdasani (2003, pp.277–278), Samuels (2018) writes:

> In his paper at the Clark University conference of 1909, with both Jung and Freud in attendance, Boas made it clear that there was no "justification for (racial) hierarchies". He also spoke against the

idea that European civilisation represented the peak towards which other races and cultures were developing.

(p.6)

The problematic evolutionary theories of 19th-century anthropology are most apparent in Freud's 1913 work, *Totem and Taboo*– a treatise that has since been heavily criticized by modern-day anthropologists for its ethnocentrism. Celia Brickman (2018) notes that within the psychoanalytic profession itself:

> Concern with Freud's use of evolutionary theory, where there has been any, has most often been confined to the "antiquated" and/or unsubstantiated nature of these elements of Freud's arguments rather than the graver issues of their racist implications. To assess Totem and Taboo as peripheral to the main concerns of psychoanalysis is to avoid reckoning with its foundational status as the origin myth of psychoanalysis and the resultant paradigmatic status of its narrative for Freud's work as a whole; and it is thus to avoid reckoning with the implications of the racial assumptions of Totem and Taboo for all of psychoanalysis.

(p.79)

Implications

Both Freud and Jung were speaking at a particular point in history within a certain cultural and social context and from linguistic assumptions that have changed. However, the term *primitive* continues to be used widely within the psychoanalytic discourse without any exploration of its roots, the possible racist implications for our thinking today and the impact on black people reading such material. While the term is etymologically neutral, its colonial pedigree means that it carries troubling connotations. I recall no point in my training or in all the years attending clinical and theoretical seminars that anyone—including myself—raised any concerns about its historic undertones. In a recent discussion with colleagues, we discovered that there were a variety of perspectives on the meaning of the word primitive including "original," "primal," "instinctive," "regressed," "violent" or even "unconscious."

It will not do to dismiss the implications of such a word that appears so frequently and with such authority in the writings of our founding fathers, both of whom were fully aware of its connections to non-European peoples and the colonial attitudes of their time. Their use of the term was intended to carry a comparative imagery for the better understanding of the European individual. This forms an important part of what we as post-Freudians and post-Jungians have inherited. Given the propensity for racist thinking in the white liberal mind, to continue to use the term without proper thought means that we risk perpetuating what at least consciously we now see as the error of their ways.

Warren Colman (2016) writes:

> While no psychoanalyst today would associate themselves with the idea of the primitive as a racial or cultural notion, it remains deeply embedded in psychoanalytic thought and, in this way, is likely to subtly entrench out-of-awareness racist attitudes amongst the psychoanalytic community. Perhaps this is one of the reasons why our record on diversity is so poor.
>
> (p.205)

Jung

The psychiatrist and political philosopher from the French colony of Martinique, Frantz Fanon (1986) turned to Jung in his search for an understanding of the human psyche to which he could relate. But as he says:

> Continuing to take stock of reality, endeavouring to ascertain the instant of symbolic crystallization, I very naturally found myself on the threshold of Jungian psychology. European civilization is characterized by the presence, at the heart of what Jung calls the collective unconscious, of an archetype: an expression of the bad instincts, of the darkness inherent in every ego, of the uncivilized savage, the Negro who slumbers in every white man. And Jung claims to have found in uncivilized peoples the same psychic structure that his diagram portrays. Personally, I think that Jung has deceived himself.
>
> (p.187)

Jung believed that, in becoming "civilized," European culture lost something important:

> Through scientific understanding, our world has become dehumanized. Man feels himself isolated in the cosmos. He is no longer involved in nature and has lost his emotional participation in natural events, which hitherto had a symbolic meaning for him. ... He no longer has a bush-soul identifying him with a wild animal.

His immediate communication with nature is gone forever, and the emotional energy it generated has sunk into the unconscious.

(1948, CW 18, para. 585)

Supposing that this "bush-soul" was to be found in the "primitive" lands of other, "un-civilized" continents, Jung made a number of visits abroad including India, the Middle East and twice to Africa. He was also interested in Native America and the impact of "Negros" in the United States.

Jung's equation between the "primitive" black other and the European repressed unconscious led to his fear that the "civilized" consciousness of the ego was always at risk of being overwhelmed by the "savage." This he believed was a particular danger where white Europeans mix with black Africans such as in colonized Africa and the United States:

> What is more contagious than to live side by side with a rather primitive people? Go to Africa and see what happens. When it is so obvious that you stumble over it, you call it going black … It is much easier for us Europeans to be a trifle immoral, or at least a bit lax, because we do not have to maintain the moral standard against the heavy pull of primitive life. The inferior man has a tremendous pull because he fascinates the inferior layers of our psyche, which has lived through untold ages of similar conditions … He reminds us—or not so much our conscious as our unconscious mind—not only of childhood but of prehistory, which would take us back not more than about twelve hundred years so far as the Germanic races are concerned.
>
> (1939, CW 10, para. 962)

The Jungian analyst Michael Vannoy Adams (1996) offers a persuasive critique of the racism in Jung's writing and suggests alternative explanations to Jung's interpretations and assumptions especially where he considers Jung mistook what relates to his personal unconscious for something archetypal and collective. For example, he reinterprets Jung's experience of an *n'goma* (drum/dance) during a 1925 visit to the Elgonyi of Central Africa (described in Jung, 1963, pp.270–272). At the height of the dance, Jung fears that it will get dangerously out of hand, so shouts and flourishes a whip in order to bring it to an end. Adams argues that Jung suffered a panic attack, equivalent to what Jung describes in another context as a "bush fear"—a fear he associates with the collective unconscious. For Adams, what happened "epitomizes the fear of the white European that to go black is to go primitive, to go instinctive, which is to go insane, which is to lose his ego—and, Jung says, to forfeit his authority" (Adams 1996, p.76). Adams suggests the concept of a multicultural imagination, which recognizes that images of collective experiences arise as much from cultural factors—which he refers to as stereotypes—as they do from archetypal factors.

In his paper "*Jung: A Racist*, Dalal (1988) highlights the racist nature of Jung's thinking when theorizing about non-Europeans, listing a number of quotes from his writing that are disturbing to the modern reader. Dalal points out that Jung refers to his fundamental concepts of the collective unconscious and individuation when commenting on other cultures and ethnicities and raises the question of whether it is enough for post-Jungians to position him in history as a man of his time, without examining the possible racist roots of these theories.

Dalal's paper was first printed in the British Journal of Psychotherapy in 1988. It took 30 years until, in 2018, an open letter was published in the same journal (Baird et al. 2018) signed by 35 Jungian analysts and academics formally responding to Dalal. The letter calls on all involved in Analytical Psychology to critique and revision theories that harm people of color and to apologize for the actual damage done. The letter has received mixed response within the international Jungian community. A critique of the arguments against it are summarized and challenged by Andrew Samuels in his 2018 article, "Jung and 'Africans': A critical and contemporary review of some of the issues."

It is tempting to contend that, like Freud, Jung was a "man of his times" and discard what is distasteful to modern ears without letting it trouble the essential concepts. While I do not argue that the racist elements in earlier writings negates all of the value of some remarkable and original thinking, I do believe that a too-easy blanking out of what were key assumptions within the origins of the theory risks an unwitting reinforcement of implicit racist structures in our own minds, as well as in the minds of others. Many modern-day Jungians argue that the concept of a *collective* unconscious, common to all humanity beneath and beyond the *personal* unconscious of the individual, means that the theory provides an antiracist structure by stressing the commonality of all humanity and offering a global connectivity, which is missing in Freudian theory. Potentially it does, but I suggest that a too complacent attitude is misplaced, and we must take care.

Intrinsic to the concept of the collective unconscious and the archetypal structures is that they are timeless, immutable and universal. And it is this theory that lies behind Jung's dogmatic assertions about

Africans and Asians, so for us to try to solve our problem by seeing Jung's statements as merely contextual and contingent is problematic. Reading some of Jung's statements about people from Africa, the Middle East, India and Mexico, one can appreciate Fanon's distaste as expressed in the quote earlier. Here Jung is speaking about a bushman hunter:

> A bushman had a little son whom he loved with the tender monkey-love characteristic of primitives. Psychologically, this love is completely auto-erotic - that is to say, the subject loves himself in the object. The object serves as a sort of erotic mirror. One day the bushman came home in a rage; he had been fishing and had caught nothing. As usual the little fellow came running to meet him, but his father seized hold of him and wrung his neck on the spot. Afterwards, of course, he mourned for the dead child with the same unthinking abandon that had brought about his death.
> (1921, CW 6, para. 403)

These interpretations of the bushman are breathtaking, not only in their content but also in their certitude. As Samuels points out, the anthropologist Paul Radin (1927), author of *Primitive Man as Philosopher*, knew Jung. He was "a colleague of Jung's, taught at the Jung Institute, and invited Jung to write a response to his work on the Trickster. He was a Jungian, but he turned a critical Jungian" (p.5).

Samuels (2018) quotes what Rodin (1927) wrote about the above quote:

> No greater distortion of the facts could possibly be imagined. And yet Dr Jung obtained this example from what purported to be a first-hand account ... (it) illustrates the unconscious bias that lies at the bottom of our judgement of primitive mentality, the unconscious assumption of the lack of differentiation and integration to be found there ... That an example like the one used by Jung should in all good faith be given as representative of the normal or even the abnormal reactions of a primitive man to a given emotional situation, shows the depth of ignorance that still exists on this subject.
> (Radin 1927, pp.39 and 63; Samuels 2018, p.6)

It seems that Jung's mind was made up and he took no notice of this challenge so the description remains. So be it. My concern now is how the consequent legacy has contributed to the making of our own minds.

The Collective Unconscious

The archetypal structures are unknowable directly and are unrepresentable. If we stay with the idea of archetypes as *predispositions*, then they are represented in the conscious mind as images that have been filtered through not only the personal but also the social, cultural and political layers. Thus, while the archetypal structure may be regarded as immutable, the form they take as *image* is dependent on the social and political context of the time. The image is *not* the archetype, and if we confuse the two, we appropriate the weightiness of the archetypal structure to support and justify unconscious prejudices. What is, in fact, a stereotype becomes fixed as if it were archetypal.

Like many others, I came to Jungian thinking in my search for a metapsychological theory that includes connection and a space for creativity and spirituality, and I continue to believe that there is much in the bones of Jung's ideas that is of value. But I have come to see that it also has the potential for application in ways that can be disturbing and dangerous. The collective unconscious is a stratum that exists at a profound level, but it is so large and so deep that I am increasingly uncertain as to the value of the idea in understanding daily personal, social and political life

Hillman (1986) argues that the Jungian theory of opposites keeps us pinned to a perspective of the world that is inevitably racist:

> Through serving the aim of self-correction, the ideas of shadow and unconscious maintain the theory of opposites and locate consciousness with light, day, bright, active etc. And so the entire modern psychological effort to raise consciousness, and the ego drafted to enact the endeavour, is one more manifestation of whiteness, perpetuating the very fault it would resolve. The project can never succeed since the unconscious it would redeem lies in the instrument of its intent; in the eye of its light.
>
> (p.46)

Taken seriously, such challenges unsettle and disturb. But they can also stimulate by jangling the mind and shaking us up and questioning taken-for-granted ways of thinking. It's a question of whether we have sufficient confidence in the robustness of the core principles of psychoanalytic and Jungian analytic theory to trust that they can withstand some rattling. If we can loosen our transference to our founding fathers and let them rest in their own era, we can acknowledge their flaws and allow the possibility of re-visioning and re-energizing our theoretical base.

Note

1 This chapter appears in part in Morgan. H. (2021). *The Work of Whiteness: A Psychoanalytic Perspective.* Oxford: Routledge.

References

Adams, M.V. (1996). *The Multicultural Imagination: "Race", Colour, and the Unconscious.* London: Routledge.

Baird, D. et al. (2018). Open letter from a group of Jungians on the question of Jung's writings on and theories about Africans. *British Journal of Psychotherapy* 34: 4673–4678.

Brewster, F. (2013). Wheel of fire. *Jung Journal: Culture & Psyche* 7 (1): 70–87. C.G. Jung Institute of San Francisco.

Brickman. C. (2018). *Race in Psychoanalysis: Aboriginal Populations in the Mind.* Oxon & New York: Routledge.

Bynum, E. (2017). *The Dreamlife of Families: The Psychospiritual Connection.* Rochester, VT: Inner Traditions.

Colman, W. (2016). *Act and Image: The Emergence of Symbolic Imagination.* New Orleans, LA: Spring Journal.

Dalal, F. (1988). Jung: A racist. *British Journal of Psychotherapy* 4 (3): 263–279.

Fanon, F. (1986). *Black Skin, White Masks.* London: Pluto Press. (First published 1952 Editions de Seuil)

Freud, S. (2009). The Interpretation of Dreams. Scotts Valley, CA: CreateSpace Independent Publishing Platform; Revised edition.

Freud, S. (1913). *Totem and Taboo: Some points of agreement between the mental lives of savages and neurotics: Vol 13. The Origin of Religion: Totem and Taboo, Moses and Monotheism and Other Works.* London: Penguin.

Gates, H. (1988). *The Signifying Monkey: A Theory of African American Literary Criticism.* New York: Oxford University Press.

Herrnstein, R. & Murray, C. (1994). *The Bell Curve: Intelligence and Class Structure in American Life.* New York: Simon and Schuster.

Hillman, J. (1986). Notes on white supremacy. Essaying an archetypal account of historical events. *Spring* 29: 58.

Jung, C.G. (1921). The type problem in poetry. In *The Collected Works of C. G. Jung: Vol. 6. Psychological Types.* London/Princeton: Routledge & Kegan Paul/Princeton University Press.

Jung, C.G. (1939). The dreamlike world of India. In *The Collected Works of C. G. Jung: Vol. 10. Civilization in Transition.* Princeton: Princeton University Press.

Jung, C.G. (1948). Healing the split. In *The Collected Works of C.G. Jung: Vol. 18. The Symbolic Life.* Princeton: Princeton University Press.

Jung, C.G. (1963). *Memories, Dreams, Reflections.* New York: Pantheon Books.

Lincoln, C. & Mamiya, L. (1990). *The Black Church in the African American Experience.* Durham: Duke University Press.

Lincoln, J. (1935/2004). *The Dream in Primitive Cultures.* New York: Kessinger Publishing, LLC.

Mudimbe, V. (1994). *The Idea of Africa*. Bloomington: Indiana University Press.
Radin, P. (1927). *Primitive Man as Philosopher*. Reprinted by New York Review of Books (2017).
Samuels, A. (2018). Jung and "Africans": A critical and contemporary review of the issues. *International Journal of Jungian Studies* 10: 2.
Shamdasani, S. (2003). *Jung and the Making of Modern Psychology: The Dream of a Science*. Cambridge, UK: Cambridge University Press.

5 Color Matters

From time to time, the racial complex is constellated in a manner and is of such a scale that it exposes what is raw and vicious and savage about this racist system we live within and we see white supremacy in all its ugliness. Often when it does, we who regard ourselves as white progressives rush to disassociate ourselves from the deed, now "othering" those white people playing out the complex in its crudest of forms, separating ourselves from its brutality and keeping ourselves pure and "good."

What if we didn't? What if we allowed ourselves to draw a line of connection between the action of the avowed racist and our own speech and actions that disturb and damage the people of color we live and work with?

Such an enactment was the murder of George Floyd killed over a $20 bill in the state of Minneapolis in May 2020. Courageously, Darnella Frazier, a high school student video recorded the whole event on her mobile phone. The recordings of how he died were deeply shocking and distressing, provoking a response from citizens of countries around the world. Refusing to see this event in isolation, and recognizing the global racist structures working beneath this killing, people—black and white—came out onto the streets to protest. For here was Cain killing his brother all over again and the response "Enough!" reverberated across our nations.

The trial of Derek Chauvin, the police officer accused of Floyd's murder, took place between March 8 and April 20, 2021. Watching the recordings of the trial and all the videos of aspects I had not seen before, I was conscious of how easily I could slip into a form of voyeurism and, in writing about it, an exploitation of suffering that was not mine. Sitting through the footage of videos from the initial arrest to the arrival of the ambulance was sickening, yet, disturbed as I was, I knew I was not watching it with the same emotional attunement, or

DOI: 10.4324/9781003025689-6

experiencing the same visceral and psychological impact as those whose bodies are black or brown. My feelings for George Floyd were of desperate concern and empathy—but I did not identify. Early on in the unfolding scene, Floyd pleaded "Don't shoot me man," as the police came to his car. I do not know such fear. Police for me—like officers of other social institutions—mean safety, not threat. His is not my story.

In a note to her consideration of the event in her paper, "Black Rage: the psychic adaptation to the trauma of oppression," Beverly Stoute (2021) refers to a March 29, 2021 CNN News report regarding the timing of the event. She says:

> News reports at the time gave eight minutes, forty-five seconds, as the time Floyd's neck was pinned by his assailant's knee. At the trial of ex-officer Derek Chauvin, however, it was revealed that Chauvin held his knee on Floyd's neck for nine minutes and twenty-nine seconds, holding his knee in place even after his victim had stopped breathing and was dead. The prosecuting attorney, Jerry Blackwell, broke down this span of time into three intervals: "4 minutes and 45 seconds as Floyd cried out for help, 53 seconds as Floyd flailed due to seizures and 3 minutes and 51 seconds as Floyd was non-responsive."
>
> (CNN News, March 29, 2021)

The apparently dispassionate demeanor of those white policemen throughout the arrest and murder is chilling. Chauvin keeps his hand in his pocket the entire time portraying casualness but also the possibility of sexual arousal. There was something about the intimacy of the act, the direct bodily contact, which held echoes of the horrors of a lynching. This was not a shooting at a distance; it involved no modern technology apart from the handcuffs and what must be a powerful inference that comes with an armed police force—"Don't shoot me man." It was a physical engagement that could have taken place at any time in the history of human combat. Yet this was no fair fight. All the power was with the white officers, and Floyd could only appeal to their humanity, which was tragically absent at that moment. The scene is not one of passion involving anger or fear or even panic on the part of the police who seem eerily calm. Just doing their job …

The ambulance's eventual arrival itself speaks of dissociation. One of the police called for it, and another rang at some stage to raise the level of emergency from Code 2 to Code 3. Yet at no point does Chauvin or the other two policemen get off the now lifeless body. Even when the paramedics arrive, we see one of them feeling for the pulse in Floyd's neck while the pressure from the knee remains despite being told to remove it. There is this chilling sense of men "going about their business" "just doing their job" regardless of the fact that a human being is dying. Watching this video, I see an extreme form of the way in which racism always operates—albeit not as explicitly—including within white liberals, our institutions and our societies. We are "just going about our business," "just doing our jobs" "just running our training organisations"… and failing to recognize or confront the suffering this might be causing. This is the privilege of whiteness.

White Privilege

The term "white privilege" is used to refer to the set of advantages inherited by those of us with a light-hued skin, which will include immunity from troubles that other groups may experience. It exists on an individual, social, organizational and institutional level. Because in other settings the term *privilege* implies wealth and power, it can lead to misunderstanding and sometimes defensive denial. For those who suffer oppression, poverty and deprivation, the suggestion that they are privileged may seem like an empty promise bearing little relationship to their lives. Nevertheless, as DiAngelo (2018) argues: "… stating that racism privileges whites does not mean that individual white people do not struggle or face barriers. It does mean that we do not face the particular barrier of racism" (p.24).

We who are white in Western countries can assume access to, and unbiased treatment by private and public institutions, confident we will be treated fairly by the criminal justice system, the health service, educational and other organizations. It means believing our dress, speech, ways of behaving are racially neutral, when in fact they are white. We see our own images in the media, in literature and the history books and take our representation there for granted. Whiteness comes with a blindfold, a free ticket, a blindness to the fact that we are also racialized subjects. It is having the luxury to fight racism one day and ignore it the next.

The fact that our whiteness is presumed and invisible to us allows us to benefit from the privilege we have inherited without having to acknowledge how our advantages depend on the disadvantage of others. Its hidden, implicit nature ensures we may remain "innocent" of how our institutions and our social structures favor us as white people ensuring that the racial hierarchy within society is perpetuated and maintained. Our inability (or refusal) to see how privileged our position is allows us not only to enjoy our racial benefits but to persist in defending them.

This form of "white ignorance," this failure to see the racist structures into which we are bound, allows us to isolate the racist act as located in individual "others" whom we may then separate ourselves from and view with distaste and condemnation. Thus we white liberals can retain our privilege whilst maintaining a view of ourselves as "good" and "non-racist." This bolsters the illusion that we are in control of our identity and exist outside of a collective dynamic. The failure to understand that we too have been racialized by a system that works to political and economic ends perpetuates a separatist position which locates both the causes and solution of racism within the individual.

We who are white are as much embedded in the structure of racism as are those of color, but we have inherited as part of that structure the benefit of blindsight. It is a benefit in that it allows us the luxury of distancing ourselves from the trauma of racism, and yet we are also blinded to key aspects of our own identity. As Linda Alcoff (2015) writes: "Whiteness is lived and not merely represented. It is a prominent feature of one's way of being in the world, of how one navigates that world, and of how one is navigated around by others" (p.9).

Shannon Sullivan (2006) stresses that

> in a raced and racist world, the psychosomatic self necessarily will be racially and racistly constituted. Race is not a veneer lacquered over a nonracial core, it composes the very bodily and psychical beings that humans are and the particular ways by which humans engage with the world.
>
> (p.24)

White Fragility

When confronted by the idea that we are complicit in systemic racism white people can become angry, defensive or hostile, all of which are aspects of what Robin DiAngelo (2011) describes as *white fragility*:

> Because White Fragility finds its support in and is a function of white privilege, fragility and privilege result in responses that function to restore equilibrium and return the resources "lost" via the challenge—resistance towards the trigger, shutting down and/or tuning out, indulgence in emotional incapacitation such as guilt or hurt feelings, exiting, or a combination of these responses.
>
> (p.58)

White fragility is *not* weakness but a means of maintaining the privilege of whiteness. This fragility takes the form of a sort of color-blindness that bypasses the realities of inequality and negates the need for addressing the consequences of disparity and discrimination. This means that we are unused to taking part in ordinary conversations about the fact of that privilege and its implications. We have nothing like the resilience of black friends and colleagues with whom honest engagement becomes fraught with our anxiety, defensiveness and denial. This "fragile" state of affairs distorts our interactions with those of color leading to, at best, misunderstanding and, at worst, abuse and retraumatization.

Conversations About Race

Because of the history and social and psychological rootedness of the racialization process for us all, whenever a black and a white person meet, racism will hover over the encounter to a greater or lesser extent like a specter at the feast. The usual stance of the white participant in the conversation is that of color-blindness, which allows us to perpetuate a perception of ourselves as "nice," but this leaves all the emotion, all the responsibility, all the work with the other.

Robin DiAngelo (2018) notes that:

> To continue reproducing racial inequality, the system only needs white people to be really nice and carry on, smile at people of color, be friendly across race, and go to lunch together on occasions. I am not saying you shouldn't be nice. I suppose it's better than being mean. But niceness is not courageous. Niceness will not get racism on the table and will not keep it on the table when everyone wants it off. In fact, bringing racism to white people's attention is often seen as not nice, and being perceived as not nice triggers white fragility.
> (p.153)

In his book *The Race Conversation. An Essential Guide to Creating Life-Changing Dialogue*, Eugene Ellis (2021) quotes from a talk by Jay Smooth, the host of a New York hip-hop show, the Underground Railroad, and a commentator on politics and culture:

> We are dealing with a social construct that was not designed to make sense. To the extent that it is the product of design, the race constructs that we live by were shaped specifically by a desire to avoid making sense. They were shaped for centuries by a need to

rationalise and justify indefensible acts. So, when we grapple with race issues, we are grappling with something that was designed for centuries to make us circumvent our best instincts. It's a dance partner that is designed to trip us up.

(Smooth, 2011, online. Quoted in Ellis 2021, p.17)

I know the feeling of awkward clumsiness when invited to take part in this dance that is "the race conversation." I know that state of being so preoccupied with an anxiety that I will "say the wrong thing" and be labelled as racist, that I lose sight of what is being said to me and, more importantly, of who is saying it. The concern is to maintain a sense of myself as "a good white person" (Sullivan 2014) rather than to address the fact that I may have done harm to another. The specific comment I have made that the other questions and challenges disappears into a morass of defensive denial or guiltiness and the opportunities for both reparation and learning are missed.

This response seems inevitable as long as we hold to this assumption that racism is an individual problem. Once we can see it as part of the cultural complex, once we understand that we have all been racialized by this crude, cruel, senseless division into "black" and "white," it becomes far clearer that no one can be free from the tropes and the stereotypes that are part of our inheritance. As whitened individuals, we certainly have work to do to see how such dynamics operate in our own minds and our relationships so that we might be more conscious and aware in engagements with others. Inevitably, we will sometimes "get it wrong," we will stumble in the dance and step on our partner's toes with our big white boots. And if they say "ouch," can we listen and apologize and learn, or do we blunder on complaining that our partner is too sensitive and has misunderstood our move?

Black Rage and White Defensiveness

James Baldwin (1998) writes:

> The history of white people has led them to a fearful, baffling place … On the one hand, they can scarcely dare to open a dialogue which must, if it is honest, become a personal confession—a cry for help and healing, which is, really the basis of all dialogues—and, on the other hand, the black man can scarcely dare to open a dialogue which must, if it is honest, become a personal confession which, fatally, contains an accusation. And yet, if neither can do this, each of us will perish in those traps in which we have been struggling for so long.
>
> (pp.724–725)

Beverly Stoute (2021) is an African American who writes about the "moral injury" caused by centuries of the injustices of slavery and of modern-day racism. This injury leads inevitably, she argues, to Black Rage as a psychologically healthy response for the person of color:

> Having developed in the particular cultural context of African American history and oppression, Black Rage as a construct also contains the superego imperative of what is right and the collective unconscious store of transgenerational traumas and defensive directives that manifests in an enduring sense of moral injury ... The rage is recruited intrapsychically to counter the attack from the racist's projection and the devaluation inflicted on the self. In this situation, the Black Rage construct does more than shield the self and the self's sense of worth. It protects the self from internalizing the devaluation of racism and, at the same time, reinforces a superego imperative that is experienced in a sense of moral injury.
> (p.270)

This alive, protective emotional response of outrage and protest is in stark contrast to the silent deadness of disavowal that is often the reaction when white people approach, or are approached by, the subject of race. Given the damage that racism does, surely the emotional construct Stoute describes is the healthier of the two. For the white individual, institution and society, the idea of Black Rage can raise fear and rejection and touches on an anxiety that may well have existed since the very beginnings of the trans-Atlantic slave trade. Throughout the centuries since, white people have been fearful that those they have subjugated would rise up and seek revenge.

I have wondered if some of the extreme responses of outrage at the pulling down of the statute of the slave trader Edward Colston in my hometown Bristol express such anxiety. Do some white people identify with the bronze effigy and fear that angry black people pushing back against centuries of oppression and mistreatment will come to topple us next? These responses suggest a misreading of the action for, as David Olusoga said in an interview for the BBC Radio 4 Today program, the issue is not the statues that can find their rightful place in our museums; it is the pedestals that are the problem.

This fear of ours needs to be acknowledged and challenged if we white people are to hear and take on the pain that is being expressed and find ways to respond that do not add to the trauma. Often, we can't or we don't. Often, we just hear the accusation of the black man that Baldwin describes and react defensively, blaming or pathologizing the person of color and returning the charge as if the moral injury is ours. In my experience, black and brown friends are remarkably careful and generous in the ways they engage in these race conversations with me as a white person. At times, they protect me from my whiteness—perhaps out of fear of what I might do by way of retaliation if they don't, and perhaps because that is what they have been taught to do from childhood.

Surely it is now time for white people to take on the work of understanding how we have been whitewashed into this dead place of disavowal, how it has done terrible damage not only to those who have been racialized as black or brown but also to us and to the relationships between us. Baldwin urges a "personal confession—a cry for help and healing" from white people. I don't believe that he means us to burden the other with the details of the racist thoughts and feelings that inevitably arise in the mind, but I do think that he is demanding that we hear the pain and the anger and the accusation of the other, that we work to see and acknowledge how we are implicated in the injury that is continually being caused and that we think seriously how we can contribute to the healing.

FANNY BREWSTER

Black Resiliency and White Fragility

It is the first year's anniversary of the murder of George Floyd. The world viewed the video of his murder due to the conscious intention of Darnella Frazier, a 17-year-old African American young woman. Let us question her fortitude in being able to tolerate the viewing of life leaving George Floyd's body. Let us see the resiliency of not only this woman but that of the cultural group of which she is a member. This is the strength of millions of Africanist people who have been acknowledged within a context of raciality while being feared, castigated and bargained for on American auction blocks. The double standard of racism has required that Black people be strong, be available to tolerate traumatic pain, have the courage to record for history the murder of a black man by a white policeman. Darnella Frazier should not have had to stand and record the heartbreaking traumatic image that she recorded on that May day in Minneapolis. Yet I believe that there is an underlying American psychological tenet that *accepts* her Black resiliency without question. I place this opposite *white fragility*.

Most early American sociological theories that included references to the African Diaspora grew from various racist beliefs. One of these continues to be that black people's bodies are stronger than those of Whites. This type of theory concludes that whiteness in White women is delicate, fragile, to be protected. This is not a new idea and has lived for centuries next to the idea of the strength of the black women's body and her ability to endure the harshest possible physical and mental treatment. Somewhere in the racial history before, during and after the murder of George Floyd, and the filming by Darnella Frazier, an unconscious ground existed for the idea of her strength and endurance. This strength of body pertaining to Black men has been noted and emphasized particularly within the field of professional athletics. Historically, black men were also used for the financial gain of the plantation system through enforced sexualized relations with Black women for procreation. The underpinning racist idea was of the hypersexuality of both black men and women. An aspect of this particular type of racism was in support of justification for enslavement of Africanist people. From the earliest days of slavery, the emphasis on the capturing of Africans was on the body—the strength and the economic necessity of Black ancestors to successfully cross the Atlantic Ocean in the hold of slave ships so they could endure the plantation fields. Author Toby Green (2020) says:

> The inscribing of violence on the bodies of the enslaved then continued at the ports of departure, where captives were branded with the mark of their "owners." Such violence was further exemplified through the account books of slave traders such as Bautista Perez, who assessed captives whom they had purchased solely on the basis of their economic impact, describing infirmities such as "swollen sides," cataracts and burns as "losses (daños)". The culmination of the violence was the Middle Passage itself, when potential losses from mortality were weighed up against profits to be gained from transporting the maximum number of captives. This reduction of human life to an economic equation was made explicit in the so-called "books of the dead": account books that listed the losses incurred through the deaths of those enslaved captives who perished on the crossing to the Americas, and in which the branding marks of the owners were written clearly in the margins, alongside the simple names of the dead.
> *(A Fistful of Shells: West Africa from the Rise of the Slave Trade to the Age of Revolution,* p.88)

At its roots, the very purpose of African American slavery, was the utilization of black bodies. Though slavery is no longer legally possible, the racialized idea of the potential dominance of blacks over whites continues. We can witness through police video cameras their fear of this dominance, played out before our eyes. This is important to remember, as we try to alleviate ourselves of retraumatization viewing the murder of George Floyd.

Within this frame of economic utilization was the need for white enslavers to seek, bargain, and purchase Africans and later African Americans, based on their capability to work American and Caribbean plantation fields. In addition, African Diaspora women were to be strong enough to have multiple pregnancies and give birth to large numbers of children, many of whom might be sold. Black ancestral women's bodies were for breeding as well as field work. David Brion Davis (2008) says the following in *Inhuman Bondage: The Rise and Fall of Slavery in the New World*:

> Slave women, including pregnant women and nursing mothers, were also subjected to heavy field labor. Even small children served as water carriers or began to learn the lighter tasks of field work, though many younger ones also played with the plantation's white children. We even have descriptions of slave children pretending to be drivers or overseers, whipping one another. That said, many slave children like Frederick Douglass did not fully realize that they were slaves until surprisingly late. But as Douglass and numerous other former slaves testified, the shock of coming to terms with a slave identity was then devastating, especially in a country that talked of liberty and equality and took such pride in disavowing hereditary titles and aristocratic status.
>
> (p.198)

During the trial of Derek Chauvin, the convicted murderer of George Floyd, the former's defense relied on speaking of the height, weight and physically fit appearance of Floyd. I was reminded of the racialized historical context of this aspect of the defense: the victim, George Floyd, was strong, easily capable of overpowering the policemen. There were four of them that day participating in the murder of George Floyd. At different times, two or more of them held George Floyd's body to the ground though he was handcuffed and had Derek Chauvin's knee on his neck. The pressure of this knee according to prosecution expert witnesses is what eventually killed George Floyd. But the concept of a strong black body was being used as Chauvin's defense. This is not unusual or unexpected. The white officers had to defend themselves.

They were at risk for being harmed that day, even as George Floyd laid on the ground, losing breath every moment.

The psychological underbelly of this narrative is that whites must protect *themselves*; otherwise, they will be hurt, killed, deprived in some way by blacks. This is the white fragility that shrouds the overpolicing and overarmed "protection" that African Americans have endured and continue to fight against in black neighborhoods. The psychological warfare that is placed on Africanist people has survived through centuries of "police protection." This protection was initially created by Northern cities such as Boston and Philadelphia for harbor and shipping security. Policing in Southern towns and plantations was in service of whites to guard *against* black people.

> In the South, however, the economics that drove the creation of police forces were centered not on the protection of shipping interests but on the preservation of the slavery system. Some of the primary policing institutions there were the slave patrols tasked with chasing down runaways and preventing slave revolts, Potter says; the first formal slave patrol had been created in the Carolina colonies in 1704.
>
> During the Civil War, the military became the primary form of law enforcement in the South, but during Reconstruction, many local sheriffs functioned in a way analogous to the earlier slave patrols, enforcing segregation and the disenfranchisement of freed slaves.
>
> ("How the U.S. Got Its Police Force",
> *Time Magazine*, May 29, 2021)

The policing by white men, and now women, with guns and tasers speaks directly to the continuous perpetuation of proposed defenselessness of these white individuals. The idea that they are likely to be overpowered and overcome by black people is still an aspect of a white fantasy that goes directly to an egoic belief and unconsciousness about white fragility held within the American psyche. Socialized racism implies that everyone who is white must and should have ways to protect themselves against people of color. Armed police in America have evolved into the physical representation of this psychological protection. The need to be safe and protected from blacks has shown itself through racist actions in various aspects of American life—segregated housing, segregated education and biased employment.

The underlying and oftentimes not so subtle narrative is that whites have something to be afraid of, and Blacks do not—even *their* lives.

The black life is not valued. I think that this also comes from colonized ideas that hold black lives as unimportant unless whites *say* they are important and then *only* within a context of white service or economic need. Slavery.

> Racial slavery became an intricate and indispensable part of New World settlement, not an accident or an unfortunate shortcoming on the margins of the American experience. From the very beginnings, America was part black, and indebted to the appalling sacrifice of millions of individual blacks who cleared the forests and tilled the soil. Yet even the ardent opponents of slaveholding could seldom if ever acknowledge this basic fact. To balance the soaring aspirations released by the American Revolution and by evangelical religion, in the First and Second Great Awakening, slavery became the dark underside of the American dream--the great exception to our pretensions of perfection, the single barrier blocking our way to the millennium, the single manifestation of national sin.
>
> The tragic result of this formulation was to identify the so-called Negro--and the historically negative connotations of the word are crucial for an understanding of my point--as the GREAT AMERICAN PROBLEM. The road would be clear, everything would be perfect, if it were not for his or her presence.
>
> *(Inhuman Bondage: The Rise and Fall of Slavery in the New World*, p.102)

Racial Symbols

The concept of white fragility has hidden within it an unspoken language of racial imagery. This imagery when pertaining to people of color are weapons of brutality that are imagined to be necessary against black people, against their bodies and many times their lives. There are degrees of racial violence exhibited against black people. Our most recent collective talks within the last few years regarding racism identifies microaggressions. These small, sometimes everyday racial "pokes," as if with an ice pick are hurtful, when accustomed to can be psychologically harmful, but not physically deadly. There are varying degrees of emotional and psychological suffering caused by the speech or physical behavioral expressions of white racism. At the far end of this spectrum of suffering is torture and physical death as experienced by George Floyd.

Within American culture, ropes have been used extensively for herding of animals, riding horses, corralling on open prairies. When white Americans moved westward further onto the stolen land of Indigenous people, the rope remained a popular means to tame and control farm animals. But before this, the rope had been popularly used in the killing of black Americans. The murder of George Floyd has been imagined in the unconscious and realized as a lynching.

The rope as symbol of anti-black racism has continued for over a century. https://naacp.org/find-resources/history-explained/history-lynching-america

White Americans can be interested, perhaps even surprised at the idea of black individuals being lynched and to the extent at which this has happened. However, this form of racist activity has not been unusual in American society and has been one of the most accepted forms of physical intimidation against Africanist people since slavery. The physical means of lynching—the rope, lives symbolically not only in the white imagination but also in racist actions. For example, Amazon in currently developing the construction of a building in Connecticut has found neck rope nooses in the building. Within the last few weeks, CNN has reported that eight nooses have been found in various locations on the construction site. www.cnn.com/2021/05/26/us/connecticut-amazon-construction-noose/index.html

There is probably not one African American who does not understand the intention and implication of numerous rope nooses hanging at Amazon's newly developing site. The white imagination that brought lynching into our consciousness as a means of racial control of black people continues to exist, and live, in a behavioral reality that threatens black men and women.

Another object that has historically been used with brutal force against people of color is the bullwhip. During slavery, this was the acceptable way of keeping enslaved African Americans from escaping slavery as a punishment for trying to escape, and intimidation against rebellion. It was used by overseers, owners, any white person to "discipline," punish black ancestors for infractions—of any kind.

The use of the whip on animals was a fact of life toward training of these animals. However, the animals were not beaten into submission, stripped of their flesh. The whip was used as a visual means to frighten them into performance. It was a signal that pain could follow if directions were not heeded. When the whip began being used on Africanist people, it was not only a visual cue as to "disciplinary" action that was to occur but rather became a weapon for tearing and marking black flesh. Black people could die under the whip. The following is spoken by a former slave in *South Carolina Slave Narratives from the Federal Writer's Project, 1936–1938*:

Master had a big plantation of several farms, near 1,000 acres or more. It was said he had once 250 slaves on his places, counting children and all. His overseers had to whip the slaves, master told them to, and told them to whip them hard. Master Calms was most always mean to us. He get mad spells and whip like the mischief. He all the time whipping me 'cause I wouldn't work like he wanted. I worked in the big house, washing, ironed, cleaned up, and was nurse in the house when war was going on. We didn't have a chance to learn to read and write, and master said if he caught any of his slaves trying to learn he would "skin them alive."

(2006, p.63)

During his trip to Africa in 1920, Jung had an experience described in his autobiography *Memories, Dreams, Reflections*:

In a village on the way from Lake Albert to Rejaf in the Sudan we had a very exciting experience. The local chief, a tall, still quite young man appeared with his retinue. These were the blackest Negroes I had ever seen. There was something about the group that was not exactly reassuring ... When the chief proposed that he give a n'goma (dance) in the evening, I assented gladly. I hoped that the frolic would bring their better nature to the fore ... Soon some sixty men appeared, martially equipped with flashing lances, clubs, and swords. They were followed at some distance by the women and children; even the infants were present, carried on their mothers' backs. This was obviously to be a grand social occasion ... In spite of the heat, which still hovered around ninety-three degrees, a big fire was kindled, and women and children formed a circle around it. The men formed an outer ring, around them, as I had once observed a nervous herd of elephants do. I did not know whether I ought to feel pleased or anxious about this mass display ... It was a wild and stirring scene, bathed in the glow of the fire and magical moonlight. My English friend and I sprang to my feel and mingled with the dancers. I swung my rhinoceros whip, the only weapon I had, and danced with them ... The dancers were being transformed into a *wild horde*, and I became worried about how it would end. I signed to the chief that it was time to stop, and that he and his people ought to go to sleep. But he kept wanting "just another one." ... And so, disregarding the chief's pleas, I called the people together, distributed cigarettes, and then made the gesture of sleeping. Then *I swung my rhinoceros whip* threateningly, but at the same time laughing, and for lack of any better language *I swore at them* loudly in Swiss German that this was enough and they must go home to bed and sleep now.

(1973, pp.270–271)

White fear, as an aspect of white fragility, can control ego awareness when taken over by a racial complex that functions autonomously. How much of this type of fear, residing within the unconscious, becomes acted out in acts of racial aggression against individuals of color? When can someone white feel psychologically "safe" enough to respect, value and not attempt to harm a person of color? This question becomes significantly important if this white individual is a part of American law enforcement and is licensed to carry a gun.

The gun has evolved into an American symbol of power, control and destruction. It is the modern-day weapon of choice for destroying human life. The number of American individuals killed by guns has escalated. In a recent story from the Washington Post came the following quote on gun violence in America: "In 2020, gun violence killed nearly 20,000 Americans, according to data from the Gun Violence Archive, more than any other year in the last two decades. An additional 24,000 people died by suicide with a gun." In considering the number of deaths of African Americans by police, a study conducted following the death of unarmed Michael Brown in Ferguson, Missouri, found that the FBI (Federal Bureau of Investigation) undercounted deaths by deadly police shootings by at least 50% of such incidences. The number of fatal police shootings every year since 2015 is more than 900.

The importance of African Americans being fatally shot by police goes to overt as well as unconscious motivations. I believe that aspects of these deaths are related to fear on the part of the police as well as potential black victims.

Most of the African Americans fatally killed by police within the last five years have died by gun violence, have been unarmed and killed while attempting to remove themselves away from police, out of harm's way.

White privilege, an aspect of white fragility—I think they reside together, supports one another as elements of a racial complex, insists that power and control must be within the realm of Whites. This idea negates blacks having any power or control. Americans have seen this exist for centuries in many racialized forms. The use of guns has been the most recent deadliest symbol of racism used in the physical killing of black men and women, and by psycho-spiritual extension of their families. The psychological trauma of black families that is caused by gun violence from armed police keeps reinforcing this symbol of white power.

Whitewash

In whitewashing, there is an unconscious desire to make good all that belongs to the culture of whiteness—sociologically and psychologically. To paint over racial truths or to lend credence to racist historical lies, to harm Africanist people and pretend that there is no legitimate need for concern, these and more characterizes the assumed fragility, privilege and symbols of American racism. With whitewashing, there is no space at the table for Africanist considerations of equity. I recently heard someone say that he did not want a place at the table—that he wanted to have the power to fly over the table, to create his own space. Perhaps this is a flight to the imaginal realm that requires more thinking about and visitation. This might allow for the emergence of new symbols that may guide us to racial equity.

References

Alcoff, L.M. (2015). *The Future of Whiteness.* Cambridge: Polity Press.

Baldwin, J. (1998). The White man's guilt. In *Collected Essays.* (Ed) Orison, T. New York: Library Classics. (Original work published 1965)

Davis, D. (2008). *Inhuman Bondage: The Rise and Fall of Slavery in the New World.* New York: Oxford University Press.

DiAngelo, R. (2011). White fragility. *International Journal of Critical Pedagogy* 3(3): 54–70.

DiAngelo, R. (2018). *White Fragility: Why It's So Hard for White People to Talk About Racism.* Boston: Beacon Press.

Ellis, E. (2021). *The Race Conversation: An Essential Guide to Creating Life-changing Dialogue.* London: Confer Books.

Federal Writer's Project. (2006). *South Carolina Slave Narratives from the Federal Writer's Project, 1936-1938.* Carlisle: Applewood Books.

Green, T. (2020). *A Fistful of Shells: West Africa from the Rise of the Slave Trade to the Age of Revolution.* New York: Penguin.

Jung, C.G. (1973). *Memories, Dream, Reflections.* New York: Pantheon Books.

Stoute, B.J. (2021). Black Rage: The psychic adaptation to the trauma of oppression. *Journal of the American Psychoanalytic Association* 69 (2): 259–290.

Sullivan, S. (2006). *Revealing Whiteness. The Unconscious Habits of Racial Privilege.* Bloomington: Indiana University Press.

Sullivan, S. (2014). *Good White People: The Problem With Middle-Class Anti-racism.* Albany: State University of New York Press.

Waxman, O.B. (2021). How the U.S. got its police force. Time Magazine, May 29, https://time.com/4779112/police-history-origins/

6 The Politics of Race

A Dream

Part way through writing a book on *The Work of Whiteness* (2021), I had a dream:

> I was helping a friend move into her new home, a cottage located deep within the rolling hills of rural England. It was a lovely day. Taking a break from unpacking boxes I stood at the kitchen window and looked out across the lush green meadows sloping away beneath me to ancient woodland below. I noticed a number of animals dotted across the fields and it slowly dawned on me that these were not the usual cows and sheep I would have expected in such terrain, but large, white polar bears. It was a sorry sight as all were emaciated, clearly starving and in distress. As I looked, a mother bear and her cub made their slow and painful way towards the cottage garden until they were close beneath me. The anguish in the mother's eyes was palpable.

The dream came at a time when my understanding of my "white" identity was undergoing something of a paradigm shift. I was starting to get how "Whiteness," like "Blackness," is a constructed concept fabricated by the indigenous people of Europe to justify the exploitation of those of faraway lands and to assert its stance of supremacy. The concept leans heavily on the archetypal associations of white as pure, innocent, spiritual, while its inevitable corollary "Blackness" evokes a sense of the dark, the dangerous and the Satanic making it the ideal container for the projection of the white shadow. Realizing as Joel Kovel (1988) puts it: "racism antecedes the notion of race, indeed, it generates the races" (pp.xiii–xiv), I was beginning to understand my white identity as a political rather than a personal assembly, albeit one with long tentacles

DOI: 10.4324/9781003025689-7

buried deep into my psyche. This does not mean I do not have responsibility for my racism—I do—but I was starting to see that individualizing the struggle is not only hopeless and ultimately ineffectual but also serves to perpetuate the system, which then remains hidden—at least from white eyes.

At first, sight the imagery of the dream is tricky. The pathos of these sad, displaced creatures is its main motif and might imply "poor white people" as if we are the real victims here. Such a position echoes that implied in some of the political rhetoric in Britain today, which is outraged by the protests against structural racism as if racism is a thing of the past and it is now we white people who are the misunderstood and abused ones. In *The New Age of Empire. How Racism and Colonialism Still Rule the World*, Kehinde Andrews (2021) writes:

> If the greatest trick the devil pulled was convincing the world he does not exist, then the proudest achievement of Western imperialism is the delusion that we have moved beyond racism, that we are in a post-racial society. We are assured that the real people losing out are not minorities, or those in the underdeveloped world, but White people are being left behind by a changing world. It is multiculturism, immigration and globalization that are all conspiring to hold White people down.
>
> (p.xxvii)

This is the very opposite of my position. I fully acknowledge the reality of the white privilege that I have inherited and the harm that racism—including mine—has done and continues to do to those who are racialized as black or brown. Nevertheless, I believe that the appearance of the white bears on the edge of death in my dream expressed something complex and difficult about the state of whiteness today.

At about the same time as the dream, I attended the remarkable retrospective at Tate Britain of the Guyanese artist, Frank Bowling. The first room of the exhibition was full of paintings of a large white swan he had seen one day on his way to his London studio. The swan was trapped in a pool of oil spilt onto the road and was frantically beating its wings and struggling to fly free.

Both the swan and the bears of the dream, like so many species facing extinction, were in profound trouble. The melting icecaps of the white tundra on which they have evolved to live has driven the bears south far from their natural habitat in search of food. They are on the edge of extinction desperately seeking sustenance. Bowling's swan is trapped in a product of the exploitation of earth's resources to feed the insatiable demand of an industrialized world for ready sources of energy.

As Andrews also states: "The West is practised through patriarchy but is built on White supremacy. It is the expansion into the Americas and the exploitation of Black and Brown bodies and resources that enabled the West to come into being" (p.xxii). The hubris of this supremacist position includes a historic disregard not only for indigenous populations across the globe but also for the natural world. A hubris that was bound, eventually, to come home to roost with the effects of planetary damage now being felt even in the richest of Western countries. White supremacy is a system in which we are all trapped— albeit with very different consequences depending on where you are positioned within it.

Pondering on Bowling's swan and the bears of the dream, I came to think of these creatures as representing something of the natural, instinctive aspect of those of us who are clustered under the rubric of whiteness that has been trashed by its determined drive for supremacy whatever the costs—even to itself. Both the paintings and the dream images felt profoundly political.

Landscape

A key element of the dream was the setting. This was the landscape of my childhood, my homeland. But lovely as it can be, I know it is shaped by and steeped in the politics of the British class system. Before the 17th century, a considerable proportion of the land was held in common until a series of Enclosure Acts over several centuries took the ancient rights of the people and gave them to the few. Nowadays, 50% of England is owned by less than 1% of its population, so that about 25,000 landowners—typically members of the aristocracy and corporations—have control of half of the land. Some of these landowners during the Brexit debate pushed the notion that "Britain was full" and so we must "take back control" of our borders. In fact, the figures show that if the land were distributed evenly across England's population, each person would have just over half an acre—an area roughly half the size of Parliament Square in central London.

This privileging of a small section of society over others is apparent in our education system so that the "elite" continues to hold power to the present day despite increasing democratization. Eight out of the 15 British prime ministers since 1945 were educated at private schools, five of these at Eton College alone. Class is always key to understanding

Britain, but race and class intersect vividly where the rolling green hills of the English countryside are part of an estate owned by an aristocratic family whose "stately home" was built from the profits of the slave trade.

In 2020, the National Trust, which owns and manages key aspects of the country's heritage, published a report that identified 93 places—about one third of all its properties—built from or connected to the spoils of slavery and colonialism. They ranged from Chartwell, Winston Churchill's former home in the southeast of the country, to Speke Hall, near Liverpool, whose owner Richard Watt traded rum made by slaves and purchased a slave ship in 1793 that trafficked slaves from Africa to Jamaica. Like owners of many other such properties, the Hibbert family in Hare Hill in Cheshire were paid about £7 million as compensation when the slave trade was abolished. John Orna-Ornstein, the National Trust's director of culture and engagement, said on the publication of the report:

> At a time when there's an enormous interest around colonialism more broadly and indeed slavery more specifically, it felt very appropriate, given that we care for so many of these places of historical interest, to commission a report that looks right across them and try to assess the extent of those colonial legacies still reflected in the places we look after today.

Not everyone agrees. The report sparked furious criticism of the trust's perceived "woke" agenda from Conservative members of Parliament and sections of the UK media. The culture secretary Oliver Dowden told museums and heritage bodies including the National Trust to "defend our culture and history from the noisy minority of activists constantly trying to do Britain down." While many supported the actions of the National Trust, many others threatened to withdraw their membership.

Much of the countryside is held as private land, but even where rural Britain is available to the public, its accessibility is not equally felt across the races. Andrew Cooper (2019) highlights a recent piece in the Guardian about "The BAME women making the outdoors more inclusive."

> The British countryside being the preserve of the white middle classes is a perception that is backed by stark figures, with ethnic minorities often deterred from heading into the outdoors due to deep-rooted, complex barriers ... Recent Sport England research identifies six barriers to participation in outdoor activities for

people from an ethnic minority background: language, awareness, safety, culture, confidence and perception of middle-class stigma.

(Parveen 2020)

Cooper (2021) suggests that a psychoanalytic perspective can be useful in understanding this phenomenon noting that "twenty five years ago ... Barry Richards, a psychoanalytic sociologist, wrote about this question ... Among white people in the English countryside he says:

> there is an almost ubiquitous element of unease in response to the unfamiliarity of a non-white presence ... it may be evident in nothing more than the intensity of the first glance ... it is very hard to identify anything in the behaviour of others which one could convincingly complain about. And yet as a white person one imagines that the non-white person is left with a sense of being different, exotic, and not quite belonging ... (Here I) will explore the nature of and the socio-historical roots of some shared phantasies (in the psychoanalytic sense of the unconscious imagination) about the homeliness—or otherwise—of the British countryside. The core of (the) argument is firstly that the countryside is experienced as a body, and secondly that it is experienced as a white body and therefore as un-homely for non-white persons
>
> (1994, 52–53)

When in the 1950s and 60s Britain sought to extend its workforce in the task of rebuilding after the war, it turned to the Caribbean colonies. There, Britain was seen as the "mother country" and that to travel here was in some sense to "go home." Most who arrived on these shores were British citizens with British passports, many were veterans of the Second World War, yet the hostile reception awaiting those who arrived in Britain, the Windrush generation, was a cruel contrast to expectations. The rapper and political commentator Akala in a series for BBC Radio 4 entitled "Natives: Race and Class in the Ruins of the Empire" (June 2021) notes that many white Britons saw these arrivals—which included Akala's grandparents—as intruders who threatened their job security and way of life: "Never mind" says Akala

> that Britain has a German royal family, a Norman ruling elite, a Greek patron saint, a Roman/Middle Eastern religion, Indian food as its national cuisine, and Arab/Indian numeral system, a Latin alphabet and an identity predicated on a multi-ethnic, globe-spanning empire.

For those who are the grandchildren of these arrivals, the body of the land of which they are full citizens is experienced not as the mother's embrace within which they can be at ease, but as a white "un-homely" body in which they are made to feel unwelcome.

In a recent BBC program "Dark Matter: A History of the Afrofuture," the artist Hew Locke describes how his homeland of Guyana was "a land soaked in blood" and speaks of his fears since childhood of devils hiding deep in the landscape. This was a place seeped in the horrors of the plantations and the agony of his enslaved ancestors. While there were enslaved individuals brought here to be servants or mascots for the gentry, there were no masses of despairing Africans arriving on our shores and no plantations of sugar cane, tobacco or cotton on British soil and the land is not so directly, so vividly, so visibly contaminated. No, the dirty work was done elsewhere; while there may not be blood in the soil, there is blood on our hands.

A Triangular Trade

Key to the trans-Atlantic slave trade was its triangularity. The side of the triangle known as the Middle Passage was formed between Africa and the Americas, and the brutality of the system was experienced with its full force at these points and during the journey between. But ships did not ply their trade back and forth between the two continents. The central players, the driving force of the entire process from the start and for centuries, were the European nations, such as Britain, positioned at the third apex of this deadly three-way relationship.

This point of the triangle, distanced as we were from the physicality of the trade, we detach ourselves from the brutality of what was going on in faraway lands and across a distant ocean, but none of it, no part of the triangle would have existed without European greed and enterprise. The "armchair titans" of early anthropology sat in their libraries and studied the reports brought back by slavers and missionaries and theorized about the inferiority of the "primitives" of Africa while they wore the cotton, smoked the tobacco and enjoyed the sugar brought back from American plantations—sugar that sweetened the tea made from the leaves extracted by indigenous laborers in Asian parts of the Empire. At the time, Britain's reach was global and devastating for many local populations while all the while, the image was maintained at home of a superior nation bringing the benefits of civilization to the "primitives" of barbaric lands. This was the "white man's burden" as articulated in Rudyard Kipling's poem of 1899.

Here, in Britain, we have a peculiar and conflicted relationship to our colonial history. We learn about our country in relation to the slave trade, but the emphasis at the collective level remains Britain's role in its abolition, in particular by valorizing William Wilberforce. Even here, we ignore the role of black activists, such as the freed slave Olaudah Equiano, in ending the trade.

Attempts to address shameful aspects of our past have led to fierce debate about the place of monuments for key figures in our colonial and slaving history. In his article for the Guardian on June 1, 2021, which argued for the taking down of all statues, Gary Younge writes:

> A more honest appraisal of why the removal of these particular statues rankles with so many is that they do not want to engage with the history they represent. Power, and the wealth that comes with it, has many parents. But the brutality it takes to acquire it is all too often an orphan.

The Dream Ending

Returning to the dream, as I watch the increasingly distressed bear stumble about, roaring in anguish as her cub clings to her fur, I feel my impotence and my despair. There is nothing, it seems, that I can do.

But then I see an RSPCA (Royal Society for the Prevention of Cruelty to Animals) truck arrive, and men and women start the slow, patient work of enticing the frightened, desperate bears into the back of the lorry so they can take them away to be treated. It was striking that the work of rescue required a collective, organized response by people with an understanding of the problem. Just as the problem of whiteness is a political one with severe implications for the individual, the "solution" if there is to be one, requires cooperative, communal action. I later learnt that the animal charity was started in 1824 by a group of Victorian men in a London coffee shop; one of those men was William Wilberforce.

We are clearly not a postracial society, and if we are ever to get close to such a state, then we white people must take on the work required to confront our history, the privileges we have inherited and the damage that has been done by our present supremacist position. We need to see how such a position has contorted and contaminated our relationships with others and with our world causing a profound debilitating sickness in us that is both physical and psychological.

FANNY BREWSTER

Slavery's Laws

Racial prejudice and discrimination are not always acknowledged as solid aspects of American society that rest within the American psyche as structural racism. Feeling perhaps more like the inner landscape of a dream. Though collective American culture has until the last decade of multiculturalism been viewed as a melting pot of all ethnic groups, this in fact has not been the case. Ethnicity continues to be an influencing factor in how children are educated in this country, who gets the best jobs, and where one can live and raise a family. This remains significant, while it is also impossible to separate one's cultural being from one's psychology. Each of us is influenced by society at large as well as by family and educational teachings—and the judicial laws of the country reinforce our societal "norms." It is not a problem that we are taught the differences that exist between ethnic groups. The problem is that we are also taught to be intolerant of these differences—racial color being the most obvious difference of note. Political activities that have been most successful in promoting racism and raciality have included ones that keep the African Diaspora from being participants in the American government—the denial of civil liberties, voting rights, holding political office and controlling community politics.

The politics of race that relates to racism in America has been a circumstance that documented and justified African Diaspora slavery and later judicial, social and economic inequities, continuing through today. Laws of record range from ones created for the capturing of Africanist individuals who attempted to run away from slavery to laws forbidding the intermarriage of individuals between black (and others of color) and white ethnic groups. There are still laws on the books that state that people of color cannot buy homes in particular American neighborhoods.

The American judicial system, from its very beginning, was focused on binding the African body to American economics through enslavement. It also must be stated that eventually American laws sought to remediate the harshness and injustice of slavery by creating laws to offset the consequences of slavery.

In the beginning of American slavery in 1619 at the sale of the first African, there was no law stating that slavery was legal. It was not until 1661 that the Virginia Assembly legally required African slaves to remain enslaved for life. Within the next decade, Africans who were enslaved were now declared "property" under the law, valued and held the same as the land of white plantation owners. Laws have been created to hold Africans to the land, to force them to return to the slave holders' land if attempting to escape and to work that land as enslaved people until they died. In October 1705, the state of Virginia passed a law that gave free reign to the killing of Africanist people. This law determined that if a black person was killed by an enslaver while being reprimanded for some committed action by the enslaved individual, there was to be no recourse for killing or maiming the slave and the enslaver was not to be held responsible in any manner. In addition, any slave who was caught running away from slavery could be killed by any white person who saw fit to do so, *not only the slave owner*. As time passed and with the increase of slave rebellions, slave laws became more hateful and fatally intentional toward black enslaved people. In the beginning, as with Virginia local laws, all the slave laws established were done through local colonial governments. These laws eventually became policies adopted by state governments such as the Virginia, Louisiana and South Carolina legislatures. They also eventually led to the denial of all simple Africanist human freedoms such as beating drums, owning livestock or leaving the plantation without the slave owner's consent.

One of the most harmful of these early slave laws was the denial of blacks to be educated in reading and writing. The intergenerational tragedy of this law has been witnessed by segregation in public education that gave little or no opportunities to blacks for removing themselves from poverty through education.

The efforts to dismantle slavery came early on and much more readily in the Caribbean than in the United States. This is often believed to have occurred because plantation owners were not as easily available to be at their remote plantations. Enslaved workers most often ran the entirety of the plantation without the presence of slave owners and with minimum overseer supervision. This time provided adequate opportunities for planning escape and destruction of plantation and whites' lives. Rebellion against slavery took shape and was energized throughout the 18th century. As these revolts continued, one island after another gained freedom. The British law eliminating slavery in all its colonies promoted revolts against slavery across the Caribbean. The British Slavery Act (1833) guaranteed the African Diaspora living on the Caribbean islands, in South Africa and in Canada, "freedom" from Britain's colonizing power. During this period, approximately 800,000 enslaved Africanist individuals who had been under British colonial rule were freed. The British government paid slave owners 20 million pounds for freeing enslaved Africanist people and for the slavers' "loss" of their human African "property."

We can only wonder with paralyzing grief at the immense irony of this "debt" payment to the enslavers of Africans and their descendants. What was due to the Africanist people?

The False Construct of Race

"Race" exists as a false construct that promotes racism against human beings. This false construct has contributed to an African Holocaust, caused a Civil War and through the racist acts of many reinforced psychological trauma. The avenues of successfully creating in different forms, a continuation of this false narrative of our being unequal in our humanity, have perpetuated a form of virulent racism that creates an archetypal centering within consciousness that is difficult to address. The healing of our racism becomes possible because there are enough of us willing to move against the shadow of racism where it presents in our society.

Not everyone is willing to engage in this way. The politics of race became more evident during the presidency of Donald Trump. This type of politics added to activating a racial cultural complex within individuals and groups. We have evidence of its outcome from tragedies such as the death of Breana Taylor and George Floyd to the politically influential rise of the Black Lives Matter political movement. White nationalism, as a movement in its own right, is focused on remaining dominant as a magnet for building political power. There is no room for individuals of color within this movement that fights to not be "canceled." Meanwhile, they seek to cancel others who do not hold to their beliefs regarding the superiority of *whiteness*.

False constructs and narratives, especially the ones that have been developed since the beginning of American slavery, rely upon the psychological trauma of unconscious processes including raciality. The possibility of a racial complex, (color complex) was considered and written minimally about by Jung 100 years ago.

The trauma of a racial complex keeps being reintroduced through racism and the racist actions delivered by individuals as well as institutions. As we review and peer into the dynamics of institutional racism, we can find that ideas of racism built on lies regarding a denigrated "Other" can be expressions of the constellation of a traumatized psychological complex that then becomes even more embedded in society's institutions.

In America, the judicial system reflects the origins of racialized laws created to serve white Americans in all the ways that society could offer. The dismantling of these laws can appear as if they will be taken out of existence for the rest of the society's existence. However, even today, we see within the political realm of the American judicial system that this can be contested. The voting rights that some African Americans and their white allies died for are still today being once again fought for within the political arena of Congress. The Voting Rights Act of 1965 brought about by the continued struggle and effort of individuals beginning from even before the Civil War has been weakened by political actions of members of Congress who do not wish to see people of color, certainly not black, and now even brown, have any power in American politics through the ballot box.

The most recent 2020 presidential election that witnessed the defeat of Donald Trump has given rise to a more powerful body of congressional legislative members who are creating local and statewide laws that deprive African Americans of the vote. The victory of Joe Biden to become president aroused a determination by many conservatives in the Republic Party to lay the ground for a return to voting restrictions against blacks that are reminiscent of the Jim Crow era. Almost every Southern state and a few in other parts of the country have seen a resurgence of political activism that seeks to formulate laws decreasing the likelihood of black people voting in political elections. This is not a secret of members of the Republican Party and their allies and is not denied by promoters of these segregationist-type voting laws.

The struggle for African American political power through equality in voting rights continues even today, as it has for more than a century.

Enactment of Racism Through Jim Crow Laws

When the Civil War came to an end, it was not the end of slavery consciousness in the American psyche. The period of Reconstruction that led to the Jim Crow era, (1876–1954), named after the characterization of black people in an imitation of vaudeville racist humor, was to have been a time of recovery and restoring the Union of the states to a more noble and worthy reunion. This did not happen because Southern enslavers felt the bitterness of the loss of economic dominance through their plantations. It also did not happen because the North felt that they, through the federal government, were required to compensate Southern enslavers and wealth holders for the loss of their "property"—land and the enslaved African Americans.

During Reconstruction, state laws were created commonly known as "generation property" or "years property," to ensure that blacks can keep their land on an intergenerational basis. The land was to remain in the family and was never allowed to be sold outside family members.

These laws were generally created following the Civil War and during Reconstruction to assure that Southern blacks would have property to which they held deeds and titles that could not be taken away. However, there is a shadow side to these laws. Even the creation of generation property has had its legal loopholes and failings that allowed whites to steal black-owned land following the Civil War.

In 1865, the federal government began creating laws to *humanize* Africanist people, beginning with the 13th Amendment to the Constitution that outlawed slavery for the entire United States. The later Amendments, 14th and 15th, claimed that blacks were American citizens with all the rights given to whites, including the right to vote. In 1875, following the enactment of these laws, civil rights laws were created that were to give assurance that blacks could stay at hotels, ride public transportation and attend entertainment available to all whites. The laws were created but following them came the *Black Codes*, then Jim Crow laws.

The laws were on the federal records, but the protection of blacks and enforcement of these laws could never exist in any way that gave blacks a true sense of more physical or psychological freedom, especially in the South. Laws without a means of enforcement and/or fought against by the law officers who were to protect blacks (they may have been *participants* of terrorism under the white hoods of Klansmen) failed to give blacks rights in the post–Civil War era. The message was clear: you can vote but you might be dead before you get back home from casting your vote.

Lynching and the rise of the Ku Klux Klan assured former Confederate soldiers, southern whites and even northern whites afraid of blacks in the years following the Civil War that blacks would be controlled by white dominance in the form of physical violence. When this failed, local and state laws countering federal laws were designed such as one in South Carolina that forbade blacks from having any employment other than servant or farmer without paying a tax. In those Reconstruction years, there was a constant harsh pull between some attempt at correcting the horror of centuries of slavery and the desire of others to return to those days of black enslavement and white dominance. Law enforcement acting as agents of American companies developed *vagrant laws* that made black men and women reactivated slaves through forced labor in mines and on farms. Jim Crow laws touched on every aspect of African American life, from where you could sit in a public transportation vehicle—"colored only," to whom you could marry—no racial intermarriage was permitted.

By 1883, the Supreme Court was once again strongly vocal in the direction of destroying civil liberties for black Americans. It was in this year that the Court declared the Civil Rights Act of 1875 unconstitutional. Following this was the major law case loss, *Plessy v. Ferguson*, determined by the Supreme Court that blacks were not entitled to sit in the same public transportation car as whites. This test case of black civil liberties, brought by African American Homer Plessy, and lost in the Supreme Court, constituted a return to pre-Civil War status for blacks once again binding them to a political status lower than that of whites and confirmed by the highest court in America.

It may appear almost irrelevant to discuss the history of these laws and their outcomes, but it is highly important in seeing the political racism that joined with the building of political institutions within our American society. This gives us a wide and even deep perspective on how the impact of political racism has harmed the African Diaspora and the collective at large. It takes us out of any denial of the interconnectedness between politics and race. It takes us into a deeper understanding of the psychology of racism that can function within the individual as well as the political structures built by such individuals—whether they be politicians, judges, police officers or American presidents.

In this book, we are seeking to deepen our own consciousness regarding a connection that is most relevant to politics, culture and good mental health. The judicial laws that guide our lives should emerge from our ideals, values and morality. How are we to persist in this American belief that is revealed to be a political falsehood as related to the African Diaspora, when we must stare without blinking at the negatively racially influenced politics of America through the centuries? A large part of healing American racism will depend on accepting the truth of an African Holocaust, recognizing the damage it has caused to the American collective cultural psyche, and setting an intention to have meaningful reparations that acknowledge the depth of harm committed over generations to those of African ancestry.

The laws that evolved in support of stolen Africanist people brought to the North American continent as slaves were meant to create human enslavement for the duration of their lives. The laws were an agreement between an economic white racialized system with black labor as its base and white law enforcement at its will. The African Diaspora were not ever free in any honest, truly spirited sense of the word.

The oppression of locally enforced laws of segregation, state and federal laws all combined during different time periods, to take away any liberties assumed with the Emancipation Proclamation. Oftentimes, the removal of civil liberties meant the death of African Americans. Terrorism was an aspect of this removal that showed itself in the numbers of blacks murdered by lynching and other means of torture. The symbols of this terrorism, Confederate statues and memorials remained long after the 1954 *Brown v. Board of Education* Supreme Court case that stated that segregation in public schools created inequality toward blacks. Meanwhile, it took the state of Mississippi until 1995 to ratify the 13th Amendment abolishing slavery.

Embodiment of Social Justice

If the African Diaspora had value because of their economic worth and were an aspect of functionality same as the land, then the political movements to save and value black people had an equally profound effect on political raciality in America. It can be said with almost great certainty that Africanist people would still be enslaved today if it were not for political movements that pushed for raising consciousness against American slavery, increasing judicial influence through corrective laws and gaining economic leverage through destruction of the Southern foundational plantation system.

References

Akala (2021). *Natives: Race & Class in the Ruins of Empire.* BBC Radio 4. www.bbc.co.uk/programmes/m000wl4m

Andrews, K. (2021). *The New Age of Empire: How Racism and Colonialism Still Rule the World.* London: Allen Lane, Penguin Books.

Cooper, A. (2021). Taking your own side in the argument. *British Journal of Psychotherapy* 37 (3): 484–492.

Green, A. (1970). The dead mother. In *On Private Madness.* London: Hogarth Press.

Harris, A. (2012). The house of difference, or white silence. *Studies in Gender and Sexuality* 13(3): 197–216.

Kipling, R. (1899). The white man's burden: The United States and the Philippine Islands.

Kovel, J. (1988). *White Racism. A Psychohistory.* London: Free Association Books.

Morgan, H. (2021). *The Work of Whiteness. A Psychoanalytic Perspective.* London: Routledge.

Parveen, N. (2020) The BAME women making the outdoors more inclusive. The Guardian. 2.12.2020.

Richards, B. (1994). *Disciplines of Delight.* London: Free Association Books.

Younge, G. (2021). *Why Every Single Statue Should Come Down.* The Guardian. 01.06.2021.

7 Concluding Thoughts

Coming toward the end of our venture together brings a mixture of emotions including both sadness and relief. It has not always been an easy engagement—but then we didn't expect it to be. I think if it had been, it would have been empty. Fanny and I first met in person a few years back when she was in London to speak at a conference with fellow African American Jungian analyst, Alan Vaughan, and I was asked to be the respondent to both. The conference had begun with an interview with Gary Younge, the then Guardian journalist, as well as a presentation by Eugene Ellis and others on the work of BAATN (Black and Asian Therapists Network). I was the first white person to speak formally, and I came at the end of the day's conference program—although Fanny gave a moving poetry reading a little later. I felt uncomfortable and anxious; the subject was charged and painful, and I worried that there was a sense "now here is the white person coming on at the end of the day to say how it is."

Following my presentation, Alan and Fanny were asked to comment on my response before the discussion opened. When the chair turned to her, Fanny was silent for a few moments and then said—I don't recall the exact words—that while she appreciated what I had said, she was always wary when a white person spoke. Wary and anxious as to what might happen next. What attack, what hurt, what unthinking racism might surface. Her comment was a powerful intervention and resonated with many of the people of color in the room. A young black woman was moved to tears. She had been ready to praise me for my "thoughtful" presentation and put aside her own anxiety, which Fanny had put into words. She had made it possible to *both* respect what I had to say *and* articulate an ever-present danger for people of color.

This event was an important experience for me. I had written that response with care and attention and spent a considerable amount of time making sure that it was as true and honest as it could be. Having

DOI: 10.4324/9781003025689-8

read Alan and Fanny's contributions beforehand, I appreciated just how much they had to cope with in managing the racism in the profession as well as generally in life. I very much wanted to use myself and my experience as a white British woman to focus on we white people and the work *we* have to do if we are to create anything close to a fair and just society and a profession that is welcoming to all. While my presentation was a response to what Alan and Fanny had written, I was mostly trying to speak to the white people in the room.

But, of course, Fanny was listening as an African American Jungian analyst, and her wariness was honest and real. I am aware that this same caution has been there throughout our writing together. Black friends tell me, however well one knows someone, however much they are trusted, if they are white there is always an uncertainty as to what careless slip, what clumsy speech or action might ambush the relationship at any moment causing hurt. Difference can never really be forgotten. Fanny and I didn't know each other personally before we started this venture although we had read and respected each other's work, and while I think we managed matters reasonably well, questions of trust were inevitably present throughout.

How Jungian Are We?

When we first discussed the project and contemplated possible differences between us, I was aware that my training had been very much in the London Developmental School as described by Samuels (1985). Fanny had had a more classical Jungian education, and I was aware from her previous books that she referred to the Collective Unconscious and the Archetypal structures more than I would. We wondered what difference this might make but, in the end, it seemed to me to be a lesser factor of difference.

Over the years, I have become increasingly troubled by some of Jung's writing on race—as I had been on his comments on women—and was wondering whether the description "Jungian Analyst" was either accurate or wanted. So, I was interested to understand how Fanny approached this question. When we discussed it, I was struck how we both shared a similar criticism of Jung and some post-Jungian writings and an attitude that might be described as healthy irreverence as well as exasperation with the failure of the current leadership of the Jungian community to take on an active and rigorous critique of some of Jung's most troubling pronouncements. I think for me, while I would welcome a different label, it does at least allow an expanse and a flexibility that can include a linking up of internal worlds with powerful external forces such as racism.

Black and White

The central disparity was one of color and therefore of ancestry and experience due to where we are each located in the power relationship that is racism. I have spoken elsewhere of how a key aspect of white privilege is that we have a choice whether to address—or even register—our whiteness and its impact on others. Racism is a matter I can ignore, deny, or disavow should I wish to. Fanny cannot.

Early on when we met on Zoom calls, I decided to keep my image on the screen next to Fanny's rather than "hide self-view" as I usually do as I needed to see on my screen what it was that Fanny looked at on hers. It is easy to forget one's own skin when talking from within it, and I needed to see the whiteness of the woman Fanny was speaking to. There were several powerful moments—some of connection and some of dissonance—especially when Fanny was talking about her ancestry and the consequent pain she lived with. It brought home to me how courageous she was in speaking to a white person who could not suffer the hurt with her as a black friend might, yet was a member of the "race" whose ancestors enslaved hers.

In a previous chapter, I described my dream of starving, displaced white bears searching the pastoral English landscape for food and how I came to see them as symbols of the destructiveness of this phenomenon "whiteness." The damage of centuries of Western exploitation of indigenous people, intertwined as it is with our blatant disregard for our planet, means that whiteness can no longer sit smugly aside and locate the problem elsewhere. There is increasing recognition across the globe that the climate emergency, patriarchy and white supremacy are inextricably intertwined as key components of the domination of the West in the Modern era. The urgency of the ecological catastrophe pushes us all to realize that the consequences of this system that reaches into every aspect of our lives can no longer be hived off as problems for indigenous groups, ethnic minorities, women ... While the suffering is by no means equally shared, it is coming to us all unless there is a radical change driven not just by people of color but by those of us who are white, who must give up our privileged ways of being if we are all to survive. This is not an altruistic move but one that is generated by the need to turn around a suicidal drive toward our own extinction. Joel Kovel (1988) puts it well:

114 Concluding Thoughts

> Racism, which diminishes its object to non-human status, also diminishes its perpetrator: all are losers by its terms. It does so, in the final analysis, by diminishing life, by reducing it to an abstraction, the better to manage it historically. And racism thereby becomes part of the wider problem of man's compact with the natural world in which he finds himself.
>
> (p.233)

The destructiveness of racism harms us all both physically and psychically. I do not in any way equate the hurt of white people with that of black people; the scales of pain and injury are not balanced. This disparity was evident in our weekly talks together. There were moments when I felt misunderstood and sometimes hurt, and I was also aware at times of a deep sense of grief at what we have lost, but these, I know, were of an entirely different order from the distress Fanny was often describing.

Mostly, the moments when I felt Fanny had misconstrued what I was saying didn't matter. Just a little hurt/pride on my part and perhaps a touch of white fragility. When I felt they were significant, I said so, and we worked with the tension this sometimes brought in. Mostly, we were laying our experience and our perceptions alongside each other, seeing how fundamentally they could differ just as our positions within this racist power structure differed. We could not pretend otherwise. I certainly can't pretend I "know" what it is like to feel the weight of the trauma of inheritance from generations of enslaved ancestors. Just as I don't know what it is like to face the racial injustices of life in a modern western country from within: our law, health, education and employment and experience of discrimination or hostility because of the color of my skin. All this sat like a heavy weight in our discussions together impacting on the relationship. There were moments when I struggled with a conflict I never resolved regarding whether I had a right to feel anger with Fanny, and when I did, should I, could I, state it directly? A mix of concern that my feelings could do damage, the usual white fear of appearing racist *and* a touch of British reserve all served to hold me back at times. While I believe that we managed as open and as deep a conversation as was possible given the circumstances and the topic, I guess we both held back for different reasons at times.

This difference in experience is always what has lain behind the moments of tension and stress in our engagement together. In one conversation, I was telling Fanny about a BBC series about a group of divers who searched the seabed for slave ships wrecked on their way from Africa to the Americas. What these men and women were seeking to find and honor were the watery graves of enslaved Africans. The program was powerful and moving. I also used the word "fascinating" about the series, and Fanny angrily responded that for her this was profoundly painful and distressing; it was not "fascinating." This very significant gulf between us broke the surface and faced me with the complexities and the pain of what we were trying to do. Clearly the word "fascinated" was thoughtless and certainly clumsy. I had been very moved by the series—as well as angry at this criminal brutality of my ancestors' complicity—but I could not feel it in the same way that Fanny does and she heard my distance. Our ancestral history has washed us up on different shores. I knew I could not—should not—lie about what I felt but how could we find a way to hold our different perspectives and keep on talking?

The United States and the United Kingdom

The other difference between us that became increasingly apparent as time went by is just how different our countries are in relation to race.

Our conversations have highlighted for me the distinct histories of the United States and the United Kingdom in relation to the triangular trade and the considerable implications racism plays out in our respective countries today. Because the plantations existed on American soil, there was a much more direct, visceral connection to the trade; the history is more visible, less easily denied or disavowed. In Britain, while there were individual slaves, there was no legalized slavery as such. We had no Jim Crow laws, no Ku Klux Klan, no lynching in the way they happened in America. The consequences of our colonialism did not hang from our trees but from those of distant lands.

Fanny writes powerfully of the noose, the whip and the gun as symbols that speak to the experience of America in relation to race and express something of the brutality of the ways one human is able to treat another that leaves deep scars running through the generations. Those living in Britain today whose origins can be traced back to the plantations of the Caribbean will carry such images—both conscious and unconscious—within the psyche. For them, the pain of historic slavery and current racism are held both in the mind and in the body as Fanny describes. This has led me to wonder what it is like for those living in Britain whose ancestors were enslaved where the accepted cultural artefacts relating to a history of slavery do not match those of trauma inherited through the generations from a dark past.

Because, for the majority British culture, the noose and the whip—while familiar and recognizable from the screen of the cinema or the television—belong to distant shores. And in Britain, we do not have the gun culture of the United States. Our police are not regularly armed, which means that—though shockingly black people do die in police custody—we have far fewer police shootings. These are not our symbols, and so I wondered what are?

When I raised the question with Fanny at the end of one of our conversations, she said, "the teacup." It made us think of the sugar served in the parlors of the British gentry sweetening the tea shipped from the British Raj in India, and the contrast—the chasm—between this image of her ancestors working the sugar plantations under the heat of the sun and the whip of the overseer, and mine thousands of miles away sipping the sweetened tea from porcelain cups. Always here, this assumption of "civilized" innocence that ignores and disavows the brutality of the trade that we were driving. Blood was spilt on other continents, not ours, and cries did not reach British ears. But it was Europeans who drove the trade and Europeans who profited. It was my ancestors who benefited from the sweat and toil and tears of Fanny's.

British culture has a reputation of suppression and repression where a truth that is difficult or inconvenient is smothered in smog made up of a blend of reserve, politeness and humor. Our dark history and current racism lurk underground or is reimagined by an assumed collective narrative. Perhaps another emblem might be that of the statues that glorify the men who were central to the running of the trade which have continued until very recently to hold their positions looking out over the centers of our cities.

A third symbol is the knife. We have experienced some years of heartbreaking events where young black men have been knifed on our streets by other black youths. These young lives are lost through violent encounters, which must be understood within the context of inherited trauma and growing up in a racist society. Unlike the gun, the knife does its work noiselessly, echoing the silence about racism that has so long existed in Britain.

End Point

The question of guilt arose at one point, and I wondered about my own. As I wrote in an earlier chapter, white guilt is a tricky business if it isn't firmly located in the depressive position thus making possible both reparation and repair. Stephen Mitchell (2000) suggests the concept of 'guiltiness' which looks similar to appropriate guile but can be dangerous in that the focus is on my own discomfort rather than the damage done to the other—who may then be required to alleviate my distress,

True, healthy guilt includes grief and mourning for damage that has been done and the subsequent change and loss in the relationship. For me, this feels a more real and "clean" emotion than guilt, and I think it is what my dream about the bears was pointing to—a terrible grief for what white supremacy has done to this world, and to relationships such as mine with Fanny. Certainly there were moments when I experienced a great sadness for the inevitable barriers between us.

When the terrible facts of our ancestral legacies and their interrelations arose in our talks together, pain and anger were always close. I could do nothing about what my ancestors had inflicted on hers, but I often felt the sense of responsibility to find some sort of reparative action. Or, at the very least, to do no more harm. I know I failed. I had to sit at times with that sense of a rather feeble liberal impotence where all I could do was to keep trying to understand.

The fundamental nature of our differences, rooted as they are in the colors of our skin and the natures and histories of our respective countries, goes deep, and we have always been working across the distance between us. This gap is one that empathy and imagination worked hard to bridge but could never close.

I recall a moment when Fanny and I were struggling to understand each other. I wondered aloud how the disparities in perception we were experiencing due to our different inheritance and different location in the racist power structure could be felt in their reality without cutting us off from each other. Fanny replied by saying that only love and relationship can get us through this. I guess it always comes down to love in the end.

FANNY BREWSTER

The Sweet and the Bitter

I began this co-authorship with Helen as a collaborative venture stepping into a difficult task that engages interweaving a narrative about ethnicity, racism, politics and psychology. The anticipated difficulty would center on the anxiety of me a black woman and her a white one writing together about raciality. Knowing this, we sought engagement that could find and provide kindness or silence when our discussions arrived directly into a realization of how our individual ethnicities kept us apart. We are both Jungian analysts, and so this was a common ground that allowed us to begin with some mutuality of understanding. Right away, one of Helen's question was: "What *kind* of Jungian analyst are you?"

That question was disconcerting to me and somewhat offsetting because even though I have this as a professional title—and it does mean more than that on a personal level, I barely think of myself *as* a Jungian analyst. Helen's question appeared to want to add another textured layer to my identification. I wondered about this because I can sometimes feel a misidentification with this professional title. I most often *imagine* the title. It can move, shape-shift, be absorbed or disappear. There are many possibilities, and this suits very well the paradoxical and porous quality of being an Africanist Jungian analyst. So Helen's almost first question to me instinctively made me want to answer: "I'm not—one." This was our beginning—somewhat unclear, and on soft, slippery ground. It closely followed our opening conversation about our possible tensions regarding writing about race. Helen's question to me was intended as an inquiry into the signature school of Analytical Psychology of which I was a member. No negative judgment was intended.

I believe that due to sensitivity to questions of identity raised by the history of racial relations, I am more likely to be more aware of and feel the tension of such a question. I am not specifically aware of the intention of seeking information regarding professional status. I am also aware of a questioning within me that directly targets inquiries of identity posed by someone white. In our work together as writers, we were and will always be faced with our ethnic differences. It would be congenial to say that these differences made Helen and I bond more easily. It sometimes created the opposite effect for me. I do believe that this was because of our topic. How does one delve into race, politics and psychology and keep a "level head" for the shared experience of writing together? I don't believe that it is possible. The emotions, as part of a racial complex, are activated throughout the experience of cowriting. We spoke via Zoom weekly having conversations of preparation and review of our separate emotional writing experiences and written material. Our differences due to ethnicity became more obvious as the months passed.

Each chapter topic required of me the necessary reflection on the major event of my writing the book: the African Holocaust, colonialism, and its continuing impact on Africanist people politically and psychologically. During our time of writing together, George Floyd was murdered. Breonna Taylor was murdered. Ahmaud Arbery was murdered. Our weekly conversations ceased to exist for what appeared to be a long while. Months went by without extended contact. It seemed like our project might fade away and never return. I know that for myself the trauma of black people being murdered was too difficult to share with a white writing partner. This was our first difference of great

Concluding Thoughts 119

substance that I noticed. It came almost at the very beginning of our writing project.

As the pandemic grew larger and more individuals died, our writing project appeared egocentric and miniscule when compared with the COVID-19 stories of those losing their loved ones.

I realize I'm writing now in this Closing Reflection about the personal moments that I lived with *and* avoided in my writing process with my co-author. An underlying realization for me is that raciality, no matter how we wish to reframe it, requires so much talking about, investigative walking around and patience. Helen and I are both interested, available, *want to* dig deep. We want unconscious material to emerge, we wanted to spend time discussing our research until it became too painful. In those times, we plowed through, or I canceled our meeting times.

I found out much more than I anticipated in doing the research for this co-authored book. The research that I had begun decades ago, in the small library in my birth hometown, culminated due to a DNA search, in my discovering that my third grandfather was a white plantation owner. This came to my attention as I worked through Chapter 4, "The Creation of the *Other*: Modern Psychology and Its Influences." Helen was waiting for the publication of her book entitled *The Work of Whiteness* while we both worked together on our book. I shared with her about my finding regarding this white ancestor, how it brought up feeling unsettling and questions regarding more about my ancestral lineage. Within me, it brought up wonderings and emotional distress as I considered the circumstances of my third grandmother pregnant with the slaver's child. I have yet to find her name or any information about her in the historical records. I don't expect to. Yes, co-authoring this book was far from what I had imagined when I first set to the task of writing my Introduction chapter.

An eerie presence within the phenomenological field came to our work in discussions of Chapter 6, "The Politics of Race."

In this chapter, I wrote about the laws of slavery, the Black Codes, Jim Crow, the segregationist bent of the Supreme Court. Helen wrote about a dream she had that felt like it was about politics and race. As we spoke about these two very different topics—dreams and the law, our conversation converged on a topic of the colonizer's triangle of rum, sugar and African bodies that fueled this economic fortune for Britain. The emergence of difference between Helen and myself grew almost palpable.

My image of a sugar cane plantation with ancestors working through the heat of *every* day was sharply pressed against the image of a porcelain cup, flowered, beautiful, *fragile*. I am deeply disturbed by the coexistence of these two images. The painful realization that there is nothing I can do to save my ancestors from this suffering. That history is just that and this was our fate and that we lived through those plantation days. We survived. Sometimes, this is not enough. As I sat looking at Helen and discussing sugar in porcelain British cups and what it took to create that moment in a British upper-class drawing room, I could not help but feel my rage.

Once during a previous talk, Helen had said, "There is no upside to the history from the perspective of African people." It was a moment when I had felt mournful of how my ancestors had suffered in those centuries of American slavery.

In our moment of the porcelain cup, I could once again feel the difference of pain and grieving on an archetypal level between us, between white and black people that requires such deep mourning that can only be reflected in a historical understanding of a holocaust on a cultural group level. Helen and I did not and would never share this. Though we had previous intellectual discussion of this very same thing, the moment had arrived for me in an embodied and emotional way. This is the feeling that comes because your ancestor has crossed the Atlantic almost buried alive in a ship among others. Imagining all the horror that has followed.

The moment when you know that it doesn't matter how much someone says *they* have suffered, and their group has also suffered. This moment you know to be singular. There is nothing else that compares.

Color and/or Colour

Helen and I shared ideas about the differences between being American and being British. This conversation first emerged because we had to decide what English language version to use in the book in terms of spelling. A simple question at first for ourselves, and then for our editor at Routledge. Out of this question grew our consideration of one of importance that caught our attention on how the cultural psyches of each country functioned in terms of race and racism. This was always a background question during and before we even began writing, but now it seemed more specific to how we lived separately as individuals in different lands. Helen spoke of how Britain's psyche lives underground—everything looks "perfect" on the outside, beautiful homes representing a clear and clean conscience. This is of course relevant to the issue of slavery and the British engagement with the slave trade. Because no widespread slavery existed in an American plantation style on British land, there is a sense of cleanliness of this sin against humanity. Ships were commissioned, built and left safe British harbors bound for the taking of human life. No impurities were apparent at the departure of white sails, the ships, leaving on their voyages. The story was of course different in the Americas and the Caribbean. Nothing but the inhuman impurity of slavery. Helen thinks that we Americans can live out much on the surface. I have heard Americans described as "wild," spontaneous, colorful—the opposite of what the British citizen wishes to be or at least presents as being.

When we moved this part of our conversation to race and racism, my questions were more as to what lingers, thrives in the American psyche in terms of race? If British society wants to keep an image of itself as "proper," "clean hands" in terms of its slavery history and racism inherent in this narrative, and give American "guilt" and all of the tragedy of slavery, how does this live in both places—in surface as well as in the underground of the American psyche?

There is no doubt that the American surface had "blood in the soil" spilled from years of its original sin of Africanist slavery and Native American genocide, to fighting its wars—Revolutionary and Civil. The level of white "madness" that actively lived for centuries during Africanist enslavement speaks to a condition that we are only now beginning to name for what it was. What ran underneath, within the American psyche, the psychological that allowed for centuries of slavery, genocide of Indigenous people? Helen spoke of "primal instincts." I then thought and spoke of her white bear dream in her writing from Chapter 6. She said that those bears and the swan cover for her book represent politics and race—they are metaphors for how "whiteness" is stuck and is dying. My image of this moment in the comparison of our two countries' psyches and cultural complexes is that America can hold both places of traumatic madness, on the surface as well as underground. White rage, the archetypal energy of sadism, greed psychosis, all run mad escaping from the underworld and can live through racial complexes that are out of control. Witness the murder of George Floyd. The caging of brown children whose Central American parents sought asylum. The vehicular killing of Heather Heyer in Charlottesville.

Helen says, "We are very different countries." I agree. Britain can now attempt to hide behind some changes in history. The slaves are freed, but the intergenerational trauma remains. America may still live out on the surface parts of its madness—gun violence massacres can happen anytime, anywhere. Maybe this American cultural complex of violence *must* act out against something as it did at the initiation against the British motherland in the 18th century. Perhaps, the violence of British colonizing is not forgotten and lives on as a haunting in the American cultural psyche. Is this an American cultural complex enactment of a British need to be hidden and without blame?

Common Ground

The effort to co-author this book on race, politics and culture has held many surprises for me. It has been my first attempt to engage in writing in this way with a co-author. The themes of the writing and the ongoing dialogues were provocative, sometimes painful and at times frustrating. I realized toward the end of our writing experience that it reminded me of a couple that goes for therapy to save their marriage. There is a fifty-fifty chance that their marriage will not survive even though their intention was to save the marriage through counseling. Helen and I did not dissolve our writing relationship. We worked through issues that were on the surface and minimally beneath. There were times that we dove deep. I don't think we could have consistently gone deeper based on the themes of race that we encountered. I was probably more defended than she was. I felt that I had/have more to protect. Our cultural histories of blackness and whiteness keeps us apart in this way. I do believe that it is partially archetypal.

How do we know what is passed on in this way due to our interconnected, historical relationship by way of our ancestors? It seems that the ego can only defend at times because the unconscious presents waves, moments of unconsciousness, that cannot be processed in the expected way. I think that these address how we must consider new ways of being with one another as regards raciality.

What is possible that does not conform to how we have been processing racialized ideas and our very existence with one another for centuries? I do believe it comes from not just ideas but also from the somatics of the body, the dreams of the unconscious, the stories of those who have lived before us. We live in a time of transition. It can possibly become transformative.

Co-authoring this book has led me to more questions regarding what lays in silence, waiting for us to develop as a different kind of being-ness, as we think about racial relations.

I did not expect this to be an aspect of any emergent experience with Helen. We were going to write a book about race and ethnicity, and I had a few clear ideas about chapters, and so on, but perhaps not so much about how the racial complex would be constellated in this process. Something that I learned more about was regarding the difficulty of being with whiteness, having to collaborate with whiteness when you are working with and through your own blackness. There seems no meeting place possible in this phenomenological field. How then do we come together in an authentic way to think about healing racial trauma? Maybe the work that is currently being done with racially separate affinity groups is more supportive, for right now. Maybe for always. Is it possible that the trauma that continues to unfold for Africanist people will take centuries to remediate in any way that feels truly healing?

White humility, black reparations and the resolution of white guilt and more will all play a part in transforming racism in America. We have conversations about these things now. It is a bare beginning. We must ask ourselves what we want. Not just for ourselves but for our children to come, for our planet. As a woman of color, a black woman, I attempt to look backwards to my ancestors, to those who suffered, survived and gave me all the goodness that they could from their bare existences. This is very important to me as a human being. What will I give and leave for those coming behind me? This must be my consideration as an elder and the descendent of African slaves. It takes effort to remember and contain in any given moment of consciousness the tragedy of my cultural group. Writing this book with Helen, a white author, has caused more purposeful thinking than I had imagined when I first began. I am still creating new places within myself to question with curiosity and to hold because of a new way of thinking about race that has emerged due to this writing project.

I don't have new answers. I didn't begin the writing project seeking new answers, only to see what might happen if I did engage on such an expedition of creativity. This was more of my journey—in the beginning, to explore creativity with another around a topic that I assumed would be challenging. The challenges continue, and I do believe that it is as it should be. Helen's question as to what kind of Jungian analyst I am returns to me now. I think I can say that the most significant aspect of being, claiming this title is because it allows me the freedom to *be*, to exist and use the inherent freedom within the title to engage with life with a forward thrust. The originating of more questions because of this writing project is promising for me and gives me some direction for future writing projects. The uncertainty of finding unknown ancestors is exciting and profoundly moving to me as a black woman.

I know less than I did when I began this co-authorship with Helen, and this points me in a direction that I believe is worthy of exploring— the difficult, ambiguous and paradoxical questions that my life offers. Hopefully, this will continue to intrigue me until the end. Helen's and my work together involving ego and unconscious is a strong aspect of the nature of how we engage with creating psychologically healthy interior spaces for ourselves and our patients as well as supporting this in the outer world—in our collective. Unknowingly, at the London conference on the day I spoke of my first African Diaspora ancestor, and Helen was the discussant, we were beginning a conversation about a deeply experienced event that touched us as present-day individuals as well as the lives of our ancestors. I hope that we have both honored our past and through our heartfelt writing and dialogues contributed to our present and future in terms of racial relationships and deepening a collective and cultural understanding in terms of psychology and politics.

References

Kovel, J. (1988). *White Racism: A Psychohistory.* London: Free Association Books.

Samuels, A. (1985). *Jung and the Post-Jungians.* London: Routledge & Kegan Paul.

Mitchell, S.A. (2000). You've got to suffer if you want to sing the blues: Psychoanalytic reflections on guilt and self-pity. *Psychoanalytic Dialogues* 10(5): 713–733.

References

Abraham, N. & Torok, M. (1994). *The Shell and the Kernel: Vol. 1*. Chicago & London: The University of Chicago Press.
Adams, M.V. (1996). *The Multi-cultural Imagination: "Race", Colour and the Unconscious*. London: Routledge.
Akala (2021). *Natives: Race & Class in the Ruins of Empire*. BBC Radio 4. www.bbc.co.uk/programmes/m000wl4m
Alcoff, L.M. (2015). *The Future of Whiteness*. Cambridge: Polity Press.
Andrews, K. (2021). *The New Age of Empire. How Racism and Colonialism Still Rule the World*. London: Allen Lane, Penguin Books.
Asante, M.K. (1998). *The Afrocentric Idea*. Philadelphia: Temple University Press.
Augustine of Hippo. (2003). *The City of God*. London: Penguin Classics.
Baird, D. *et al.* (2018). Open letter from a group of Jungians on the question of Jung's writings on and theories about Africans. *British Journal of Psychotherapy* 34: 4673–678.
Baldwin, J. (1998). The White man's guilt. In *Collected Essays*. Orison, T. (Ed.). New York: Library Classics. (Original work published 1965)
Brewster, F. (2013). "Wheel of fire". *Jung Journal; Culture and Psyche* 7 (1): 70–87. C.G. Jung Institute of San Francisco.
Brewster, F. (2017). *African Americans and Jungian Psychology: Leaving the Shadows*. London: Routledge.
Brewster, F. (2019). *Archetypal Grief: Slavery's Legacy of Intergenerational Child Loss*. London & New York: Routledge, Taylor & Francis.
Brewster, F. (2020). *The Racial Complex: A Jungian Perspective on Culture and Race*. London & New York: Routledge.
Brickman, C. (2018). *Race in Psychoanalysis: Aboriginal Populations in the Mind*. London & New York: Routledge.
Bynum, E. (2017). *The Dreamlife of Families: The Psychospiritual Connection*. Rochester: Inner Traditions.
Colman, W. (2016). *Act and Image: The Emergence of Symbolic Imagination*. New Orleans, LA: Spring Journal.
Cooper, A. (2021). Taking your own side in the argument. *British Journal of Psychotherapy* 37 (3): 484–492.

References

Dalal, F. (1988). Jung: A racist. *British Journal of Psychotherapy* 4 (3): 263–279.
Davis, D. (2008). *Inhuman Bondage: The Rise and Fall of Slavery in the New World*. New York: Oxford University Press.
DiAngelo, R. (2011). White fragility. *International Journal of Critical Pedagogy* 3 (3): 54–70.
DiAngelo, R. (2018). *White Fragility: Why It's So Hard for White People to Talk About Racism*. Boston: Beacon Press..
Diop, C.A. (1987). *Precolonial Black Africa*. Chicago: Lawrence Hill Books.
Drayton, R. (2005). The Empire Pays Back. Review. London: The Guardian. 20.8.2005.
Duncan, D. (1998). *Calendar: Humanity's Epic Struggle to Determine a True and Accurate Year*. New York: Avon Books.
Ellis, E. (2021). *The Race Conversation: An Essential Guide to Creating Life-changing Dialogue*. London: Confer Books.
Fanon, F. (1986). *Black Skin, White Masks*. London: Pluto Press. (First published 1952 Editions de Seuil)
Federal Writer's Project. (2006). *South Carolina Slave Narratives from the Federal Writer's Project, 1936-1938*. Carlisle, MA: Applewood Books.
Freud, S. (2009). *The Interpretation of Dreams*. Scotts Valley, CA: CreateSpace Independent Publishing Platform; Revised edition.
Freud, S. (1913). *Totem and Taboo: some points of agreement between the mental lives of savages and neurotics: Vol. 13. The Origin of Religion: Totem and Taboo, Moses and Monotheism and Other Works*. London: Penguin Books.
Frosh, S. (2013). *Hauntings: Psychoanalysis and Ghostly Transmissions*. London: Palgrave Macmillan.
Gates, H. (1988). *The Signifying Monkey: A Theory of African American Literary Criticism*. New York: Oxford University Press.
Gottlieb, A. (2004). *The Afterlife Is Where We Come From: The Culture of Infancy in West Africa*. Chicago & London: The University of Chicago Press.
Grazine, G. & Murray, S. (Eds.). (2014). *Confronting Cultural Trauma: Jungian Approaches to Understanding and Healing*. New Orleans: Spring Journal.
Green, T. (2020). *A Fistful of Shells: West Africa from the Rise of the Slave Trade to the Age of Revolution*. New York: Penguin Books.
Gyekye, M. (1987). *An Essay on African Philosophical Thought: The Akan Conceptual Scheme*. Cambridge, UK: Cambridge University Press.
Harris, A. (2012). The house of difference, or white silence. *Studies in Gender and Sexuality* 13 (3): 197–216.
Hartman, S. (2007). *Lose Your Mother: A Journey Along the Atlantic Slave Route*. New York: Farrar, Straus and Giroux.
Hazlewood, N. (2004). *The Queen's Slave Trader: John Hawkyns, Elizabeth I and the Trafficking in Human Souls*. London & New York: Harper Perennial.
Herrnstein, R. & Murray, C. (1994). *The Bell Curve: Intelligence and Class Structure in American Life*. New York: Simon and Schuster.
Hilliard, C.B. (Ed.). (1998). *Intellectual Traditions of Pre-Colonial Africa*. Boston: McGraw-Hill.

References

Hillman, J. (1986). Notes on White supremacy: Essaying an archetypal account of historical events. *Spring* 29–58.
Hirsch, A. (2019). *Opinion*. The Guardian. 23.10.2019.
Jung, C.G. (1921). The type problem in poetry. In *The Collected Works of C. G. Jung: Vol. 6. Psychological types*. London/Princeton: Routledge & Kegan Paul/Princeton University Press.
Jung, C.W. (1939). The dreamlike world of India. In *The Collected Works of C. G. Jung: Vol. 10. Civilization in Transition*. Princeton: Princeton University Press.
Jung, C.G. (1948). Healing the split. In *The Collected Works of C.G. Jung: Vol. 18. The Symbolic Life*. Princeton: Princeton University Press.
Jung, C.G. (1963). *Memories, Dream, Reflections*. New York: Pantheon Books.
Kaufmann, M. (2017). *Black Tudors: The Untold Story*. London: Oneworld.
Kimbles, S. (2014). *Phantom Narratives: The Unseen Contributions of Culture to Psyche*. Maryland: Rowman & Littlefield.
Kipling, R. (1899). "The White Man's Burden: The United States and the Philippine Islands". Definitive Edition (Garden City, New York: Doubleday, 1929).
Kovel, J. (1988). *White Racism. A Psychohistory*. London: Free Association Books.
Lincoln, C. & Mamiya, L. (1990). *The Black Church in the African American Experience*. Durham: Duke University Press.
Lincoln, J. (1935/2004). *The Dream in Primitive Cultures*. New York: Kessinger Publishing, LLC.
Lorde, A. (2018). *The Master's Tools Will Never Dismantle the Master's House*. London: Penguin Random House.
McKissack, P. and McKissack, F. (1994). *The Royal Kingdoms of Ghana, Mali, and Songhay: Life in Medieval Africa*. New York: Henry Holt and Company.
Metzl, J. (2009). *The Protest Psychosis: How Schizophrenia Became a Black Disease*. Boston: Beacon Press.
Miller, J.C. (2012). *The Problem of Slavery as History: A Global Approach*. New Haven & London: Yale University Press.
Mills, C. (1997). *The Racial Contract*. Ithaca: Cornell University Press.
Mitchell, S.A. (2000). You've got to suffer if you want to sing the blues: Psychoanalytic reflections on guilt and self-pity. *Psychoanalytic Dialogues* 10 (5): 713–733.
Morgan, H. (2002). Exploring racism. *Journal of Analytical Psychology* 47, 567–581.
Morgan, H. (2014). Between fear and blindness. *Thinking Space: Promoting Thinking About Race, Culture, and Diversity in Psychotherapy and Beyond*. Ed: Lowe, F. London. Karnac.
Morgan, H. (2021). *The Work of Whiteness. A Psychoanalytic Perspective*. London: Routledge.
Morrison, T. (2007). *Beloved*. London: Vintage. (First published 1987)
Mudimbe, V. (1994). *The Idea of Africa*. Bloomington: Indiana University Press.

Nobles, W.W. (2006). *Seeking the Sakhu: Foundational Writings for an African Psychology*. Chicago: Third World Press.

Oduyoye, M. (1972). *The Vocabulary of Yoruba Religious Discourse*. Ibadan: Daystar Press.

Parveen, N. (2020) The BAME women making the outdoors more inclusive. The Guardian 2. 12.2020.

Radin, P. (1927). *Primitive Man as Philosopher*. Reprinted by New York Review of Books (2017).

Richards, B. (1994) *Disciplines of Delight*. London: Free Association Books

Rogers, G.C. (1985). *The History of Georgetown County, South Carolina*. Columbia: University of South Carolina Press.

Samuels, A. (1985). *Jung and the Post-Jungians*. London: Routledge & Kegan Paul.

Samuels, A. (2018). Jung and "Africans": A critical and contemporary review of the issues. *International Journal of Jungian Studies* 10: 2.

Schwab, G. (2010). *Haunting Legacies; Violent Histories and Transgenerational Trauma*. NY: Columbia University Press.

Segy, L. (1976). *Masks of Black Africa*. New York: Dover Publications, Inc.

Singer, T. & Kimbles, S. Eds. (2004) *The Cultural Complex. Contemporary Jungian Perspective on Psyche and Society*. Hove & New York: Brunner-Routledge.

Shamdasani, S. (2003). *Jung and the Making of Modern Psychology. The Dream of a Science*. Cambridge: Cambridge University Press.

Stoute, B.J. (2021). Black Rage: The psychic adaptation to the trauma of oppression. *Journal of the American Psychoanalytic Association* 69 (2): 259–290.

Sullivan, S. (2006). *Revealing Whiteness: The Unconscious Habits of Racial Privilege*. Bloomington: Indiana University Press.

Sullivan, S. (2014). *Good White People: The Problem With Middle-Class Antiracism*. Albany: State University of New York Press.

Unsworth, B. (2012). *The Quality of Mercy*. London: Windmill Books.

Walvin, J. (2007). *A Short History of Slavery*. London & New York: Penguin Books.

Waxman, Olivia B. (2021). "How the U.S. Got Its Police Force". Time Magazine, May 29, https://time.com/4779112/police-history-origins/

Younge, G. (2021). *Why Every Single Statue Should Come Down*. The Guardian. 01.06.2021.

Index

Abraham, N. 45, 47
Adams, M. V. 75–76
Africa: of antiquity 15–22; Egypt separated from 16–17; Ghana in history of 17–19; growth of Islam in 18–19; Nigerian art and 19–21; writings of European "explorers" of 66–67
African American mythology, spirituality and the dreamlife 68–71
African ancestors: beliefs regarding existence of life force energy 38; binding legacy of 34–41; theory of "being" 38–39
African Diaspora, the 21–22, 36, 39, 59–60, 104; social justice and 110
African Holocaust 4, 21, 36–37, 106; mourning and melancholia over 47–48; transgenerational transmission of trauma and 44–45
Afrocentric Idea, The 20–21
Afterlife Is Where We Come From, The 35
Akala 101
Akan peoples 38–39
Al Bakri 17–18
Alcoff, L. 84
Analytical Psychology 3, 4, 65, 67; failures of 5
Andrews, K. 98–99
Aquinas, T. 24–25
Arbery, A. 118
Archetypal Grief: Slavery's Legacy of Intergenerational Child Loss 45

Aristotle 23
art, African 19–21
Asante, M. K. 20–21

Baldwin, J. 86, 88
Bantu Philosophy 66
Bell Curve: Intelligence and Class Structure in American Life, The 67
Biden, J. 107
Bidisha 25
Black Church in the African American Experience, The 69
Black Death 24
Black Lives Matter political movement 106
Black Rage 86–88
"Black Rage: the psychic adaptation to the trauma of oppression" 82
Black resiliency 88–92
"Black Tudors: The Untold Story" 25
Boas, F. 72
Bowling, F. 98–99
Brewster, Fanny 1–6, 10, 111; ancestors of 1–2, 34–41; on Black resiliency and white fragility 88–92; conversations with Helen Morgan 113–115, 117–122; on the dreamlife 64–71; on false construct of race 106–107; finding common ground with Helen Morgan 122–124; as Jungian analyst 1, 3–4, 112–113, 117–118; on mirroring the transference 56–62; on racial complex 52, 56–62; on racial symbols 92–95; on racism

enacted through Jim Crow laws 107–110; segregation in early life of 2–3; on slavery's laws 104–106; transcript of conversation with Helen Morgan, April 20, 2021 28–32; on transgenerational transmission of trauma 45; on the triangular slave trade 102–103; Unpublished Manuscript/ *Journey the Middle Passage: Poems* 33; on whitewashing 96
Brickman, C. 27, 73
Brown, M. 95
Brown v. Board of Education 110

Catholic Church 24
Chauvin, D. 81–83, 90
Christian Crusades 24, 27
Christian missionaries 66
Civil War, American 2, 91, 106, 107; Jim Crow laws after 107–110
Collected Works 59
collective unconscious 78
Colman, W. 74
Columbus, C. 27
Confronting Cultural Trauma: Jungian Approaches to Understanding and Healing 60
consciousness hierarchy 64
Cooper, A. 100–101
COVID-19 virus 59, 119
cultural complex 44–45
cultural universality 64

Dalal, F. 9, 76
"Dark Matter: A History of the Afrofuture" 102
Davis, D. B. 90
DiAngelo, R. 10, 11–12, 41, 51, 83, 85
Diop, C. A. 17, 19
disavowal of whiteness 52–56
Douglass, F. 90
Dowden, O. 100
Drayton, R. 42
Dream in Primitive Cultures, The 65
Dreamlife of Families, The 70
dreams: African American mythology, spirituality and 68–71; Jungian analysis of 64–68; of politics of race/racism 97–103
Duncan, D. 35

Egypt 16–17
Ekpenyon, O. 48
Eliade, M. 66
Ellis, E. 85–86, 111
"Empire Pays Back, The" 42
Enclosure Acts 99
Equiano, O. 103
Europe: acceptance of slavery in 22–25; Black Death in 24; feudalism in 23–24; legacy of slavery for 41–46; rise of color racism in 25–27; triangular slave trade 102–103
European Holocaust 44, 45, 47

Fanon, F. 74
feudalism 23–24
Fistful of Shells: West Africa from the Rise of the Slave Trade to the Age of Revolution, A 89
Floyd, G. 58, 81–83, 88–93, 106, 118, 121
Frazier, D. 81, 88–89
Freud, S. 65, 67, 71–72; reliance on early anthropologists 72–73
Frosh, S. 44

Gates, H. 69
Ghana 17–19
Gottlieb, A. 35
Grazine, G. 60
Green, T. 89
guiltiness 46, 56, 116–117
Gyekye, K. 38

Harris, A. 46
Hawkyns, J. 26
Heyer, H. 121
Hilliard, C. B. 16
Hillman, J. 71–72, 78
Hirsch, A. 48

Ibn Khaldun 17
Idea of Africa, The 66
individuation 10–11

Inhuman Bondage: The Rise and Fall of Slavery in the New World 90, 92
Intellectual Traditions of Pre-Colonial Africa, The 16
Interpretation of Dreams, The 65, 67
Islam 18–19; Christian Crusades against 24

Jim Crow era 107–110
Jung, C. G.: early work of 65; Freud and 65; interest in dreams 65, 67–68; reliance on early anthropologists 72–73; theory of a Collective Unconscious 64; writings about Africanist peoples 67, 75–78, 94–95
Jung: A Racist 9, 76
Jungian psychology 1, 3–4, 9, 35–36, 37, 112–113; collective unconscious in 78; dreams and 64–68; Transference in 56–62

Kaufmann, M. 25
Kimbles, S. 44–45
Kipling, R. 103
Kovel, J. 97, 113–114

Levi-Strauss, C. 66
Levy-Bruhl, L. 66, 68
Locke, H. 102
Lorde, A. 3–5
lynching 93, 108

Masks of Black Africa 20
Master's Tools Will Never Dismantle the Master's House, The 4–5
McKissack, F. 15–16
McKissack, P. 15–16
Memorial 2007 48
Memories, Dreams, Reflections 67, 94–95
Metzl, J. 59
Miller, J. C. 22, 42–43
Mills, C. 50
Mitchell, S. 46, 116
Morgan, Helen 3, 6–11; background of 7–9; on black rage and white defensiveness 86–88; on the collective unconscious 78; on conversations about race 85–86; conversations with Fanny Brewster 113–115, 117–122; on disavowal of whiteness 52–56; finding common ground with Fanny Brewster 122–124; on Freud and Jung's use of anthropology 71–73; on guilt 116–117; on individuation 10–11; as Jungian analyst 1, 3–4, 9, 112–113; on Jung's search for scientific understanding 74–77; on landscapes of race 99–102; on legacy of slavery 41–44; on politics of race/racism 97–103; self-examination by 9–10; on the term *primitive* 73–74; transcript of conversation with Fanny Brewster, April 20, 2021 28–32; on white fragility 84–85; on "Whiteness" and "Blackness" concepts 11; on white privilege 83–84; work with therapeutic communities 9, 50–52 mourning and melancholia 47–48
Mudimbe, V. 66

Nazism 59
New Age of Empire, How Racism and Colonialism Still Rule the World, The 98
Nigeria 19–21
Nobles, W. W. 36, 38–39

Oduyoye, M. 21
Orna-Ornstein, J. 100
"Other," the 1, 4, 56, 58, 61, 106

Parveen, N. 100–101
phantom effect 45
phantom narratives 45
Plato 23
Plessy v. Ferguson 109
politics of race/racism 6; landscapes of 99–102; Morgan on 97–104; slavery's laws and 104–106; triangular slave trade and 102–103
Powell, E. 7
Precolonial Black Africa 17
primitive, use of term 65–66, 73–74, 75
Primitive Man as Philosopher 77

Problem of Slavery as History, The 22, 42–43
projection 57–58, 62
Protestantism 68–69
Protest Psychosis: How Schizophrenia Became a Black Disease, The 59

Quaker movement 25, 48
Quality of Mercy, The 43

race: conversations about 85–86; false construct of 106–107
"Race and Psychoanalysis" 27
Race Conversation. An Essential Guide to Creating Life-Changing Dialogue, The 85–86
races, emergence of idea of 26–27
racial complex 50–52; disavowel of whiteness and 52–56; exposing racism 81; mirroring the transference and 56–62
Racial Complex: A Jungian Perspective on Culture and Race, The 45
racial symbols 92–95
racism 113–114; conversations about race and 85–86; different histories in the United States and United Kingdom 115–116, 120–122; economics and 5; enacted through Jim Crow laws 107–110; pain of recognizing 62; phantom effects and 45; politics of 6; rise of color 25–27; skin as culture and 37–38; white fragility and 10–12, 84–85; white privilege and 83–84
Radin, P. 77
recognition of difference 55
Richards, B. 101
Rogers, C. 64
Royal Kingdoms of Ghana, Mali and Songhay: Life in Medieval Africa, The 15–16

Samuels, A. 10, 72, 76, 77
Schwab, G. 45, 47
Seeking the Sakhu: Foundational Writings for an African Psychology 36, 38–39

Segy, L. 20
serfdom 23
Shamdasani, S. 72
Signifying Monkey, The 69–70
Singer, T. 44–45
skin as culture 37–38
slavery: African ancestors legacy of 34–41; in ancient Greece 23; Black resiliency and 89–90; European acceptance of 22–25; legacy of 41–46; mentioned in the Bible 24; mourning and melancholia over 47–48; physical abuse in 92–95; politics of race and laws of 104–106; in the Roman Empire 23; transcript of Fanny/Helen conversation on, April 20, 2021 28–32; triangular trade 102–103
Smith, L. 11
Smooth, J. 85–86
social justice 110
social mythology 68
South Carolina Slave Narratives from the Federal Writer's Project, 1936–1938 93–94
spirituality, African American 68–71
Stalinism 44
St. Augustine of Hippo 24
Stein, M. 60
Stoute, B. 82, 87
Sullivan, S. 84
symbols, racial 92–95

Taylor, B. 106, 118
Torok, M. 45, 47
Totem and Taboo 66, 73
trans-Atlantic slave trade *see* slavery
Transference, the 56–62
trauma, transgenerational transmission of 44–45
Trump, D. 106, 107
Truth, S. 68
Tubman, H. 68

Unsworth, B. 43

Vaughan, A. 111–112
Vocabulary of Yoruba Religious Discourse, The 21

Walvin, J. 25–26
white defensiveness 86–88
white fragility 10–12, 84–85, 88–92
White Fragility: Why It's So Hard for White People to Talk About Racism 11–12, 41
white ignorance 50, 84
whiteness, disavowal of 52–56
white privilege 83–84

whitewashing 96
Wilberforce, W. 48, 103
Work of Whiteness, The 97
Wragg, A. 40
Wragg, S. 2
Wragg family plantation 2, 39–41

Yoruba traditions 69–70
Younge, G. 103, 111

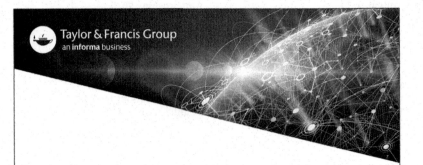

Taylor & Francis eBooks

www.taylorfrancis.com

A single destination for eBooks from Taylor & Francis with increased functionality and an improved user experience to meet the needs of our customers.

90,000+ eBooks of award-winning academic content in Humanities, Social Science, Science, Technology, Engineering, and Medical written by a global network of editors and authors.

TAYLOR & FRANCIS EBOOKS OFFERS:

- A streamlined experience for our library customers
- A single point of discovery for all of our eBook content
- Improved search and discovery of content at both book and chapter level

REQUEST A FREE TRIAL
support@taylorfrancis.com